Translating Literature: Practice and Theory in a Comparative Literature Context

Translating Literature

Practice and Theory
in a Comparative Literature Context

André Lefevere

The Modern Language Association of America
New York   1992

© 1992 by The Modern Language Association of America
All rights reserved
Printed in the United States of America

MLA and the MODERN LANGUAGE ASSOCIATION are trademarks owned by the
Modern Language Association of America. For information about obtaining permission
to reprint material from MLA book publications, send your request
by mail (see address below) or e-mail (permissions@mla.org).

Library of Congress Cataloging-in-Publication Data

Lefevere, André. Translating literature : practice and theory
in a comparative literature context / André Lefevere
pages cm. — Includes bibliographical references and index.
ISBN 978-0-87352-393-6 (cloth) — ISBN 978-0-87352-394-3 (pbk.)
1. Translating and interpreting. I. Title.
PN241.L353   1992
418'.02—dc20   92-20469

Seventh printing 2016

Published by The Modern Language Association of America
85 Broad Street, suite 500, New York, New York 10004-2434
www.mla.org

Contents

Preface for the Instructor   1

Preface for the Student   3

Chapter 1. Translation Studies   5

Chapter 2. Language   15

Alliteration   20
Allusion   22
Foreign Words   29
Genre   31
Grammatical Norms   35
Metaphor   37
Names   39
Neologisms   41
Off-Rhyme   42
Parody   44
Poetic Diction   49
Pun   51
Register   58
Rhyme and Meter   70
Sound and Nonsense   75
Syntax   78
Typography   80
Word and Thing   82
Works Cited   83

Chapter 3. Text   85

From Passage to Text   86
The Four Levels of Translation   86
Ideology, Poetics, Universe of Discourse   87
Text: Catullus 32   89
Text and Ideology   90
Text and Poetics   91
The Cultural Status of the Text
    and the Passage of Time   92
Translation Strategies   94
The Weight of Traditional Interpretations
    of Writers and Their Texts   95
Translation Tactics: The Illocutionary Level   97
Conclusion   108
Works Cited   111

Chapter 4. Context: The Function of Translation in a Culture   113

From Text to Context: Categories for
    Further Analysis   114
Audience   115
Authority   116
Image: Culture   125
Works Cited   131

Chapter 5: Literary Translation and Beyond   133

Chapter 6. Topics for Classroom Teaching and Research

Chapter 6. Topics for Classroom
Teaching and Research   141

Suggestions for Further Reading   147
Index   163

Preface for the Instructor

This book provides a possible structure for the many courses in literary translation increasingly offered in comparative literature departments, language departments, and English departments. It deals with the two aspects of the study of literary translation: process and product. Chapter 1 sets forth general observations about the field of translation studies. Chapters 2 and 3 discuss the process, or the actual production of translations of literature. Chapter 4 explores the role the finished product plays in the receiving literature and culture and stresses the great importance of translation in the evolution and interaction of literatures and cultures. The inclusion of both aspects allows instructors and their students not just to concentrate on challenges arising during the translation process but also to integrate the study of translation with that of literary theory and comparative literature in the analysis of the role played by the finished product. I therefore suggest that equal time be given to these three chapters.

Chapter 2 lists challenges translators are likely to encounter on the subtextual level, that is, on the level of style, rhetoric, and culture-bound elements in the original. Each type of challenge is briefly identified and commented on. The chapter then presents examples of each type. Instructor and students may attempt to confront the challenges, or they may simply want to discuss them and point out the difficulties likely to beset such attempts. Finally, in most, though not all, cases, a maximum of two examples of solutions discovered by published translators are given for comparison, analysis, and commentary.

Since courses in literary translation offered in literature and comparative literature departments tend to attract students from different linguistic and cultural backgrounds, I avoid using language-pair-specific examples. All examples in this book are given in English, accompanied by literal translations where necessary.

The challenges listed in English should, therefore, be supplemented by the students themselves with challenges in other languages. Students from different linguistic and cultural backgrounds should look for similar or analogous challenges in their own traditions and present them to class, together with literal translations and fairly extensive commentaries.

Chapter 3 lists challenges that confront the translator on the textual level. Some subtextual challenges identified in chapter 2 reappear, of course, but attention is focused on the possible matching of genres, forms (text types), and worldviews. After the students, along with the instructor, have worked through the text presented here, they should look for different translations into English of seminal works belonging to their own literatures. They should present those in class, again with literal translations and commentaries, and describe the strategies used by the translators. They are also encouraged, though not required, to try to translate the original text themselves.

Chapter 4 focuses on and expands the other aspects of literary translation: the role played by translations in the receiving literature and culture. If the instructor and the students pause to reflect that translations are texts that refer to and claim to represent other texts, they will find themselves linking translation studies with literary studies and cultural studies in general. Another moment of reflection leads to the insight that the teaching of literature makes use of other kinds of texts, besides translations, that refer to other texts and represent them, such as anthologies, histories of literature, or criticism. Together with translations, these other "rewritings" are to no small extent responsible for the image of a writer, a work, or even a literature that is presented to both students of literature and the reading public.

Students should work through the text of chapter 4 and then look for an instance of a rewriting of a famous text or author belonging to their own literatures. Once again, they could present instances of such rewritings in class. Chapter 6, "Topics for Classroom Teaching and Research," offers ideas and guidelines for the construction of such presentations, which can be expanded to papers or even dissertations.

Finally, "Suggestions for Further Reading" lists most of the important contributions to the field of literary translation and cultural communication published in Europe and the Americas during the last three decades.

Preface for the Student

This book introduces two aspects of the study of literary translation: process and product. If you are primarily interested in the study of the translation process, mainly because you want to try to translate yourself, you are likely to be helped more by chapters 2 and 3. If your interest lies in the role played by types of texts, such as translations, that claim to refer to and represent other texts in the evolution and interaction of literatures and cultures, you will find that aspect addressed in chapter 4. However, you will probably discover that these concerns overlap and that you will, therefore, profit equally from all three chapters.

Chapters 2 and 3 discuss different challenges that arise in the course of the translation process. Discussion of these challenges is not designed to provide you with general, rulelike solutions, not least because the transitory, historically limited nature of such solutions becomes very obvious in chapter 4. Rather, you are asked to identify the different types of challenges and to devise solutions for them. To help you do so, solutions devised by other translators are also listed in chapters 2 and 3. Once you have worked with the English-language examples, you are encouraged to look for examples of similar challenges in your own language and literature, to provide them with literal translations and commentaries, and to present them in class for analysis and discussion.

Working through chapters 2 and 3 will not turn you into an accomplished translator overnight. No course can do that, certainly not in a limited period of time. Rather, these chapters seek to sensitize would-be translators to the issues involved. Those of you who do not want to translate yourselves will find that chapters 2 and 3 not only help you to read existing translations in a different manner but also bring the concerns of chapter 4 into sharper focus.

Chapter 4 deals with the very powerful influence that translations and other "rewritings" (texts that refer to other texts and claim to represent them) exert not just on the way literatures and cultures are received but on the very way in which literature is taught. Because the study of translations and other rewritings inevitably uncovers the mechanisms of canonization, integration, exclusion, and manipulation that are at work on many levels—not just of literature, but of society—it acquires relevance beyond the realm of literary studies. Suggestions for pursuing these issues further are listed in chapter 6, "Topics for Classroom Teaching and Research."

After completing a course based on this book, you can go on to produce translations, to analyze translations and rewritings produced by others, or both. Whatever you decide to do, you will have found that the study and the production of translations and other rewritings of literature is a central concern of literary and cultural studies today.

Chapter 1

Translation Studies

From republican Rome onward, translation has been used in language teaching in the European educational system. Though the practice has for some time been abandoned, its long dominance has helped define thinking on translation in Europe and the Americas. It has defined that thinking mainly in terms of "right" or "wrong," "faithful" or "free," and other rigid categories. It did so because institutions (the church, the state and its educational system) were interested in ensuring that the books most often translated were translated in the "right" way, that the translations of, say, the Bible and the Greek and Roman classics were "faithful." Such a tradition is forced to neglect all kinds of other aspects connected with the phenomenon of translation, a circumstance that could teach us many things about how cultures and literatures function.

This book tries to deal with translation in a way that goes beyond right or wrong. In this introduction, I try to explain why, and I also try to show that the approach I advocate can incorporate older approaches, complement them, and make them more fruitful for future research. I must first ask the reader to imagine the translation of literature as taking place not in a vacuum in which two languages meet but, rather, in the context of all the traditions of the two literatures. It also takes place when writers and their translators meet, an encounter in which at least one of the parties is a human being, made of flesh and blood and provided with an agenda of his or her own. Translators mediate between literary traditions, and they do so with some goal in mind, other than that of "making the original available" in a neutral, objective way. Translations are not produced under perfect laboratory conditions. Originals are indeed made available, but on the translators' terms, even if these terms happen to produce the closest literal (faithful) translation.

Having made this statement, I immediately need to amend it: translations may be made on the translators' terms, but those terms are not necessarily their own. Translators, too, are constrained by the times in which they live, the literary traditions they try to reconcile, and the features of the languages they work with.

Translators are the artisans of compromise. Paradoxically, this position gives them the kind of power that is wielded most effectively by the ostensibly weak. Since they are at home in two cultures and two literatures, they also have the power to construct the image of one literature for consumption by the readers of another. They share this power with literary historians, anthologizers, and critics. The production of translation is an activity sui generis; the study of translations should be subsumed under the more encompassing heading of rewriting. Translators, critics, historians, and anthologizers all rewrite texts under similar constraints at the same historical moment. They are image makers, exerting the power of subversion under the guise of objectivity.

For a long time, thinking about translation in the West was primarily normative for the reasons I have indicated. Around the 1930s, and more obviously after World War II, with the publication of the first works by Eugene A. Nida in the United States and Andrei V. Fedorov in the Soviet Union, the focus of thinking about translation began to shift away from literary texts, but the thinking itself, interestingly, remained normative.

When translation thinking began to shift away from literary texts, it began to look toward linguistics. Most of the early "textbooks" on translation read like a rewriting of the dominant linguistic theories of the time, including some that lacked direct relevance for translation. With hindsight, it is clearer why linguistics-based translation thinking could never fully satisfy translators and translation scholars. Theories of linguistics deal with language as an abstract system, the Saussurean "langue," whereas translators and translation scholars are interested in language in concrete use, the Saussurean "parole." Even though many translators and translation scholars were, seemingly for a very long time, willing to agree with linguists that a sentence like "John loves Mary" expressed more or less the same idea as a sentence like "Mary is loved by John," they eventually stopped waiting for further revelations, based on those insights, that would be of strikingly productive use to them in their own field.

The dominant concept in this first phase of linguistics-based translation thinking was that of equivalence, which was gradually to lose its authority over the next forty years. It is not hard to see that any approach to translation dominated by equivalence is likely to focus on the word as the unit of translation, since words can be pronounced equivalent to other words more easily than sentences can be pronounced equivalent to other sentences, paragraphs to other paragraphs, or texts to other texts.

The technique of "componential analysis" was developed by Nida to gauge the degree of equivalence between words and to ensure their correct translation. Words were split up into their components. The most famous example associated with the technique—one is tempted to say unfortunately, because it fails to do justice to the method's complexity—is that of "bachelor = male + unmarried." This technique is still perfectly useful to—and used by—translators and translation scholars today. In fact, it is one of a few linguistics-based concepts that have proved to be of immediate relevance for both the production and the study of translations.

Another concept introduced by Nida turned out to be much more controversial: the concept of "dynamic equivalence," which attempted to define a translation as the closest natural equivalent to the original. The three key words—closest, natural, and equivalent—have given rise to unending controversy. Moreover, the concept of dynamic equivalence is mostly message-oriented (it was developed to ensure that the message of the Bible would be "faithfully" translated into other cultures) and thus is less useful for literary translation, which concerns not just the message but also the ways in which that message is expressed.

Whereas Nida's thinking on translation mainly involved rule giving, other linguists, such as John C. Catford, focused on the very possibility of rule giving. They essentially reduced the study of translation to the study of translatability. Instead of looking at existing texts, literary or nonliterary, and describing what they saw, they tried to establish criteria against which translations were to be judged. Needless to say, these criteria were primarily based on equivalence. They were also completely ahistorical. It is doubtful, for instance, whether passages from Martin Luther's translation of the Bible, which helped change the face of Europe forever, would qualify as a translation in Catford's sense of the word.

Not only were these criteria ahistorical, they were also completely context-free. Perhaps the best way to explain this point is to quote the famous counterexample to Nida's famous "bachelor = male + unmarried." That counterexample is "pope," which fits Nida's definition of "bachelor" but is somewhat more than that. This realization, in the summation of hindsight, is what froze the first linguistics-based attempts at thinking about translation on a level they could not go beyond and what proved in the end to have limited relevance to translators and translation scholars: a sentence is always "somewhat more" than a string of equivalent words, and a text is always "somewhat more" than a string of equivalent sentences.

Small wonder that the second phase of linguistics-based thinking about translation focused on text linguistics. The unit of translation for text linguistics is no longer the ideal contextless sentence but the text as such. Text linguistics also sees the text not as an isolated verbal construct but as an attempt at communication that functions in a certain way in a certain situation or culture and may not work with the same degree of success in another situation or culture. The robust "Don't mess with

Texas," for instance, might not go over well in certain parts of the British Isles, where the inhabitants are more used to something like "Don't litter." Incidentally, it is precisely the function and situation and culture that ensures that listeners-readers perceive these two utterances as having similar meanings. By no stretch of the imagination can "litter" be pronounced equivalent to "mess with Texas."

Text linguistics therefore adds a much-needed functional dimension to the analysis of the translation process and the analysis of translated texts. This dimension is of the utmost value for literary translation. Unfortunately, prominent text linguists like Katharina Reiss and Juliane House have not altogether been able to free themselves of the normative mind-set that characterizes Western thinking about translation. Text linguists who study translation feel almost invariably called on to come up with some kind of typology of texts. These typologies are just as invariably more or less sophisticated variations of Karl Bühler's "archetypology" that distinguishes among "representational" texts (concentrating on what is said), "expressive" texts (concentrating on the speaker), and "appellative" texts (concentrating on whoever is spoken to).

Besides being of rather doubtful relevance (each of the text types will have to exhibit some features of the others), typologies of this kind are inevitably marred by gray areas that detract from both the elegance of the theory and its applicability. They also draw an unwarrantedly sharp line between "literary" and "nonliterary" texts. They seem to postulate the existence of an ethereal verbal construction that uses only literary elements (what those might be is seldom specified) and that is then excluded from further analysis because it is "too complicated" at the present stage of research. Anybody who has ever read even a few chapters of *Moby-Dick*, for instance, will agree that parts of this work, regarded as nothing if not literary, might, with only slight modifications, figure in a nineteenth-century American textbook on whaling. It would be much more productive, therefore, to see the distinction literary/nonliterary not in absolute terms but rather as the two extremes of a scale. Various texts would then take up various positions on that scale.

Text-linguistics-based thinking about translation has not found a satisfactory way out of the dilemma in which it has maneuvered itself by both introducing the functional element in translation production and analysis and refusing to let go of the concept of equivalence in one variation or another. House, for instance, wants a translation to "function" as the "equivalent" of its source text in a different culture or situation—"no smoking" would therefore be the functional equivalent of the German "Rauchen verboten"—but she also wants the translation to use equivalent pragmatic means to achieve this functional equivalence, in which case the German *Rauchen,* being an infinitive, would not be equivalent to the gerund *smoking,* and *no* would certainly not be an equivalent of the German past participle *verboten* 'forbidden.'

Peter Newmark admits the existence of the dilemma by distinguishing between "semantic" and "communicative" translation. Semantic translation belongs more in the realm of equivalence: it tries to supply an equivalent semantic content for words found in the source text, and it concentrates more on the meaning of the source text. Communicative translation, by contrast, is more or less equivalent to a "cultural adaptation" of the source text, so that readers in the target culture find it easier to read. It deals with the message of the original, and it obviously falls into the category "functional." One cannot help but think that the dominance of the concept of equivalence has greatly contributed to the stagnation of thinking about translation.

The main problem with equivalence is, of course, that translators and translation scholars cannot agree on either the kind or the degree of equivalence needed to constitute real equivalence. It therefore seems that it's time to abandon the concept altogether, as more and more contemporary writers on translation (such as Mary Snell-Hornby) are doing, since equivalence, they claim, has become so vague that it hardly denotes anything anymore or, conversely, that it denotes all things to all people. It is in this avatar that equivalence takes its final bow in the writings of Gideon Toury. His version of equivalence effectively atomizes the concept. There are no longer any absolute criteria for equivalence, nor should equivalence necessarily be defined in general terms. Rather, Toury postulates, a construct can be found that is the "adequate" translation for every given original. This "tertium comparationis" is the objective yardstick that makes possible meaningful comparison between the original and the translation. But this "tertium comparationis," though claimed to represent the ideal adequate translation in abstract terms, is in reality a construct in the translation scholar's brain, a construct that claims objectivity while reflecting the scholar's own insights, prejudices, shortcomings, limitations, wishes, and hopes. In fact, the scholar can be said to become the norm.

Along with, and somewhat opposed to, linguistics-based approaches to translation, the period from the 1930s to now has witnessed the emergence and elaboration of the "hermeneutic" approach to translation. Even though translation scholars working in this vein use insights acquired by linguistics-based thinking, they see the phenomena translation and translator in a totally different light. To them translation means interpretation, and the translator is the mediator between two texts, no longer the finder of equivalences. In Newmark's terms, translators with this orientation produce communicative rather than semantic translations. The scholar most closely associated with the rebirth of hermeneutic studies of translation is of course George Steiner. Yet he, too, does not escape from the objections raised against the hermeneutic approach as a whole: that it is and remains obstinately vague, that it gets bogged down in the psychological process of translation, and that it never manages to forget its theological origins, which tend to manifest themselves alternately in rousing appeals and pious platitudes, not necessarily reducible to the world of common sense. Paradoxically, perhaps the most productive insight generated by this school of translation studies is the conclusion that no perfect translation is possible. If that is so, acceptance or rejection of translations in a given culture may well have much more to do with power and manipulation than with knowledge and wisdom.

Alternatives to both linguistics-based and hermeneutic approaches to translation have been elaborated over the past two decades by scholars like Anton Popovic, whose thinking tends to be more tributary to the linguistic approach, and Itamar Even-Zohar, who has been influenced mainly by literary theory, particularly the writings of the Russian formalists in their later, historical-relativistic phase. Both seek to reverse the normative mind-set that has long characterized Western thinking about translation. Instead of trying to prescribe what a translation should be, Popovic calls for a descriptive study of existing translations that can be considered one variant of metatext among others (such as the summary, the review, the paraphrase, the adaptation). Even-Zohar sees translation as a process of negotiation between two cultures: translation is acculturation. Following in the footsteps of the Czech scholar Jiri Levy, both also describe the translation process not primarily in terms of following and applying rules but as a decision-making process: translators decide, on their own, on the basis of the best evidence they have been able to gather, what the most effective strategy is to bring a text across in a certain culture at a certain time. Translation has come of age. Studying it is not a simple specialty. Students of translation need knowledge of linguistics, literary history, literary theory, and cultural history. The study of translation does not compartmentalize: it unifies. It does not leave scholars and students happily tending little plots of their own: it forces them to survey, question, examine the lay of the land time and again. The text of a translation has often been called a culture's window on the world. So is the study of translations, which marshals in its service many of a culture's most vital elements.

This book subscribes to the thesis that translation is indeed acculturation. It rejects the finality of the old normative approach, while gratefully incorporating the legacy of some of its techniques, such as componential and functional analysis. Freed from the obligation to give rules for translating and criteria to judge translations by, it claims three areas for the study of literary translation: process, product, and reception. It does not slight the study of nonliterary translation in any way: concentration on one aspect of a phenomenon does not imply any value judgment. In fact, this concentration is imposed on the present writer by little else than a certain personal predilection combined with the very salient fact that life is short.

Moreover, the study of literary translation seems to be coming into its own again in departments of literature and comparative literature in both East and West, or, rather, it appears to be groping toward some kind of understanding of what its role and its goals could be. This book tries to contribute to that understanding.

If translation is acculturation, the phenomenon can be approached from two angles that can be complementary but do not have to be. Translation can teach us about the wider problem of acculturation, the relation among different cultures that is becoming increasingly important for the survival of our planet, and former attempts at acculturation-translation can teach us about translation. Studies in literary translation focus of necessity on literature and the evolution and interpretation of literatures as part of the wider area of acculturation.

Although the second chapter of this book deals with actual translation, it does not give rules or check language proficiency. Translators should already know the languages and the cultures into and out of which they want to translate; how else can they produce meaningful work in the acculturation zone that is their real field? Rather, chapter 2 confronts potential translators with problems of acculturation that have been repeatedly encountered and offers previous attempts to solve them. Writers cannot tell prospective translators how to translate; all they can do is make translators aware of the problems and of the necessity to devise solutions. Translators can be guided by examples of strategies that have been successful in the past, as well as by examples of strategies that have failed in the past. They may decide to imitate the former and eschew the latter. Alternatively, they may decide to resuscitate the latter in a slightly altered form, if they are convinced their present situation warrants this course of action.

Chapter 2 is the longest, since it deals with problems commonly encountered during the process of translation. These problems are conveniently isolated for discussion and, eventually, attempts at solving. Chapter 3 reminds potential translators that the problems treated in chapter 2 occur within a given text, that they are not context-free, and that given texts are also not context-free: they are produced (and reproduced) within the confines of a given literature, which has its own generic and stylistic features and which is, in its turn, embedded in a whole culture. Potential translators therefore need to learn to proceed from the top down, that is, from the culture to the text to the structure of that text to paragraphs, lines, phrases and words or, if you prefer, from the macro to the micro level. On the micro level translators can use all the linguistic and hermeneutic techniques they have learned, but the finality of their endeavor is the text as part of the culture, not the much vaunted struggle with the word, the sentence, or the line. For this reason potential translators need to learn about the conditions or constraints—ideological, poetological, sociocultural, linguistic—under which texts come into being and the potentially different constraints under which they are to be translated. Chapter 3 therefore discusses strategies of transposing texts, not words or phrases, from one culture to another.

Translation studies can be a locus, disciplinary or institutional or, ideally, both, where translators of literary texts are trained, where they are familiarized with problems and taught to devise strategies. Translation studies can also be a locus for the study of existing translations and other forms of what Popovic calls metatexts and I call rewriting. Studies of existing translations can teach us much both about the process of acculturation as it takes place in translation and about strategies used by our predecessors with varying degrees of success. But we can go even beyond that: much of the influence exerted by one literature on another, or on others, has been exerted in the form of one rewriting (translation, anthologization, historiography, criticism) or another. Translations and other rewritings have also often been used as weapons in the struggle between two rival poetics: Did not the imagists claim that they "happened" to write just like the Chinese poets of the T'ang dynasty? Did they not publish themselves in anthologies, while rewriting the history of English poetry in ways that suited them? Did they not write criticism that ridiculed their adversaries?

In addition, the way we now teach literature owes a tremendous debt to rewritings: Who has read both Sophocles and Chikematzu in the original? Who has read all the works that "should be read" in their entirety rather than in extracts in anthologies? Who has never reproduced criticism without reading the work criticized? Rewriting therefore exerts an enormous influence not only on the image one literature is given of another but also on the image members of a culture are given of their own and other literatures. It is the hidden motor behind literary evolution and the creation of canons and paradigms.

Rewriting is simply a cultural given of our time. The images of a literary work created by translations and other rewritings are far more likely to attract "nonprofessional" readers than the work's strength or venerability as an original is, no matter how much professors and students of literature—the "professionals"—may regret this state of affairs. It is therefore important that the image of a work of literature and the texts that constitute that image be studied alongside its reality. This procedure represents the future of a productive study of translation integrated into comparative literature and literary theory.

If a work of literature is not rewritten in one way or another, it is not likely to survive its date of publication by many years or even many months. It is also a fact of literary life in our day that works of literature not rewritten in either English or Russian do not stand a great chance of being included in any canon of world literature, no matter how high their intrinsic value as literature may be rated. This situation invests rewriters of literature with a certain amount of power. Translators, critics, historians, anthologizers, professors, and journalists can project positive or negative images of a text, a writer, or a literature. The power of these rewriters should be analyzed, as well as the various ways in which they tend to exercise it. If it is analyzed seriously and comprehensively, it will tell us much about the influence of power and ideology on creation and education—one of the main issues of our time. Ways of studying rewriting seriously and comprehensively are therefore suggested in the fourth chapter of this book.

Chapter 2
Language

Since texts are written in language, it stands to reason that the linguistic aspect of translation has traditionally attracted most attention. Yet many decisions translators make to deal with problems on the level of language originate not on that level but on one of the hierarchically higher levels—ideology, poetics, universe of discourse, language—discussed in chapter 3. For the present, though, it is enough to keep this information stored in the backs of our minds as we proceed.

A language preexists its speakers or writers; that is, writers and translators are born into a language with its rules and conventions. They do not invent them. Sometimes they succeed in bending or adapting them, especially when they are trying to write in a lighter vein. I have therefore selected many examples for this chapter from anthologies of so-called light verse. Similarly, to show how translators have confronted challenges in the past, I have taken examples from a century and a half of translations of Aristophanes's *Lysistrata* and of Catullus's second poem, the well-known invocation of Lesbia's sparrow. Yet writers never bend language to such an extent that it becomes unrecognizable to the reading audience—unreadable, in short.

Grammatical rules and conventions may differ widely between languages, and even more widely between linguistic families, such as the Indo-European and the Dravidian (encompassing the south of India, Sri Lanka, and parts of Malaysia). It is relatively impractical to try to impose the rules of one language on another, especially when the source language is considered much more prestigious than the target language. In the past translation has been used to "educate" the target language until that language was judged to have reached the level of excellence achieved by the source language. The following lines from Samuel Butler's "Hudibras" refer to the phenomenon in question and to the negative reaction of a reading public that feels its language has completed its education by now:

> 'Twas English cut on Greek and Latin,
> Like fustian heretofore on satin.
> It had an odd promiscuous tone,
> As if h' had talk'd three parts in one
> Which made some think when he did gabble
> Th'had heard three labo'rers of Babel.
>   (Ewart 110)

Such considerations hardly obtain today. Instead, translators feel relatively free to switch grammatical categories to express what they need to express in a way the target audience finds easy to understand.

Language is also the expression and the repository of a culture. Many of its words refer to a reality that no longer exists: things and concepts die, but the words used to express or denote them may survive for centuries or just decades. "Hokeypokey," a brand of cheap ice cream sold in the United States in the 1920s, no longer exists, but the word still does. It has even taken on the additional meaning of nonsense.

Because language is the expression of a culture, many of the words in a language are inextricably bound up with that culture and therefore very hard to transfer in their totality to another language. In British English, for instance, you can say to someone, "I think you were born at Hogs Norton," and mean that the person spoken to has no manners. If you have to translate the phrase into another language, it is easy to convey its semantic information content, namely, "no manners." It is difficult, if not impossible, to literally (faithfully?) render its "illocutionary power." Often, something of that power can be conveyed only by the judicious use of analogs in the target language. Prospective target languages would not use the medieval name of a little village in Oxfordshire to express "no manners." But they may well have an expression, closely linked to the language, that renders the same semantic information content and has analogous illocutionary power. Its illocutionary component is, however, likely to be semantically quite different from a name like "Hogs Norton."

In what follows we shall deal with problems that arise during the translation process on the "illocutionary" level; that is, the level of language usage on which language is used primarily for effect. Illocutionary use of language is by no means limited to literature. "Nixon's the one" is an ill-fated example of the illocutionary use of language outside literature, as is that other slogan, advertising razor blades, "It's the cut that counts." But the illocutionary use of language tends to be more concentrated in texts usually thought of as literary.

We shall not be dealing with the "locutionary" level of language use, that is, the type of language use that results in the production of well-formed, grammatically correct sentences. Serious students of translation should have reached this level, and they should be able to go beyond it before they undertake the study of translation. The illocutionary use of language raises all kinds of problems, and not all of them can be solved without further knowledge of the context of a given passage, or even the whole text from which the passage has been taken. Translators hardly ever translate just words or sentences; they translate "chunks" of text, which become their so-called units of translation. In practice, translators translate chunks that they feel are neither too long nor too short or that they feel otherwise comfortable with. But they do not translate these chunks in isolation: they always refer back and forth between the chunk they are working on and the concept of the text as a whole that they keep somewhere in their heads while translating. That concept not infrequently makes them go back and retranslate or at least revise chunks they worked on earlier.

Ideally, therefore, students of translation should be presented with bigger chunks of texts than those given here, or even with whole texts. This is plainly impossible, for reasons of space, but it is also less useful, because it is good to develop a sense for the problems discussed here, to be able to spot them, and to deal with them. After a while, translators develop their own patent solutions for most of these problems, but they can never be sure those solutions work for all instances of the problem; the solution used in a chunk of text always needs to be evaluated against the text as a whole—and often against the target culture's assumptions about the world and about literature. Compilers of dictionaries cannot possibly foresee all the contexts in which a word they define will be used. Translators cannot possibly anticipate all the configurations of texts in which problems will arise. That is why there are no hard and fast rules for translating. The best that can be done is to teach students of translation to identify and recognize problems, to adopt solutions, and to check those solutions against the text as a whole, the "universe of discourse" (things, concepts) referred to in that text, and the poetics and the ideology of a culture at a given time.

Solutions are also based on two more considerations that should be kept in mind as we attempt to solve the problems listed below. Historically, translators have vacillated between producing translations dictated by the shape of the source text and translations designed to match the ideological and "poetological" expectations shared by readers in the target culture. The first type of translation has traditionally been called "faithful," the second type has traditionally been called "free." It is very hard, however, to find either type in its pure form. Translations of Greek and Latin poetry made during the last century, for instance, attempted to stay close to the meter of the original and to render the information contained there, but they were usually also produced in rhymed verse, even though the originals did not rhyme. The attempt to render the meter and the information would therefore fall under the heading of faithful translation, while the production of rhymed verse would fall under the heading of free translation (even though the translators themselves would not have seen it that way at the time), since the translation superimposes the poetological expectations of the target audience on the original and adapts that original accordingly. The poetological expectations of that audience could be said to be, It is not poetry if it does not rhyme. Thus translators made their translations rhyme even though the original did not.

In making decisions, translators should remember that their first task is to make the original accessible to the audience for whom they are translating, to mediate between their audience and their text. Ideally, they should be able to convey both the semantic information content of the source text *and* its illocutionary power. In practice, they can nearly always satisfactorily render the first, but not always the second. If they are to mediate effectively between their audience and their texts, they have to attach greater importance to the poetological and ideological expectations of the target audience than to the poetological and ideological considerations that influenced the production of the source text. When in doubt, translators are well advised to tilt to the target audience and its expectations, not to the source text.

This advice should not be interpreted as a blank check given to translators to do with the source text as they please. The information content of the original is generally transferable. As for the illocutionary use of language, translators have to ask themselves what part each instance of illocutionary language use plays within the framework of the text as a whole and what similar or analogous illocutionary devices are at their disposal to match that instance.

These guidelines are, I believe, about the only rules that can be given for translating, for two reasons hinted at in chapter 1. One is that rules change over the years; nowadays Greek and Roman poetry is being translated into unrhyming verse. No rules can be formulated as absolute. The other reason is that no one rule is valid for all possible language pairs. A much more productive approach is to alert translators to problems arising on the illocutionary level of language use and to trust them to cast about in their minds, languages, and cultures for illocutionary equivalents.

A second factor likely to influence translators' decisions is the absence of any monolithic audience. In practice, translators translate not for all potential readers "out there" but for a subaudience likely to be interested in a given translation. Until about the middle of the nineteenth century, for instance, many of the educated people in Europe were bilingual, or even multilingual, and would, accordingly, read translations less for their information content than present-day readers do. In the same century, emergent nations in Eastern Europe, such as the Czechs, translated from more "prestigious" languages (German, in this case) just to show that it could be done, that Goethe could be made to

speak Czech and that Czech therefore had a right to take its place as
an equal in the community of European languages. A similar phenomenon has of course been observed in the Renaissance, when Latin and
Greek were translated into German, French, and English. Needless to
say, translators translating for this type of subaudience could be forgiven
for feeling justified in attaching much more importance to illocutionary
language use than to the information content of the original.

Conversely, translators may find themselves translating for a subaudience of scholars, who are mainly interested in the information content of the original. In that case, they may decide to attach less weight to
illocutionary language use in the interest of increased direct intelligibil-
ity. Translators of *Gulliver's Travels* tend to translate in a different way for
an audience of children than for an audience of adults. There are, for
instance, very few translations made for children that allow Gulliver to
extinguish the fire raging in the Lilliput imperial palace the way he does
in the original: by urinating on it.

Bearing all this in mind we can now turn to the actual problems arising in the translation process on the level of illocutionary language use.
To show how widespread these problems are, the examples have all been
taken from five randomly selected anthologies, three of light verse and
two of prose. The anthologies are identified in the text. For quick reference, the problems have been listed in alphabetical order.

Alliteration

The repetition of the same sound at the beginning of consecutive words
has a long and venerable ancestry in most European languages. Though
usually used in verse, it can also be found in prose, as in the following
example taken from Stella Benson's short story "The Man Who Missed
the Bus": "The dog's paw hooked in a pathetically prehensile way
around his ankle" (Karl 371).

The alliterative sound here is clearly represented by the letter *p*: in
"paw," "pathetically," and "prehensile." The alliteration gives emphasis
to particular words and a certain rhythm to the sentence. Translators
should ask themselves whether it is necessary, desirable, or vital to reproduce these two features. No matter what their answer is, they will realize that the translation problem raised by alliteration is an obvious
one: it may be possible to match the sound in other languages, but not
the meaning, or, alternatively, the meaning, but not the sound.

Translators have to decide where their priorities lie and why. Obviously, translators do not make these decisions in a contextual vacuum as

is suggested here. Rather, their decisions are part of an overall strategy they develop to translate the text as a whole. These strategies are discussed in detail in chapter 3.

Just as obviously, it is by no means sure that alliteration plays a comparable role in literatures written in non-Indo-European languages. Translators into those languages have to decide whether alliteration does play such a role and whether it should be introduced into the literature written in those languages or matched with stylistic devices more endemic to that literature, especially if those devices function analogously to alliteration in Indo-European literatures.

Students should discuss the problems raised by a possible translation of the following examples. If they want to translate the examples, they should explain what they have done and why.

First, another example of alliteration in prose, from Joseph Conrad's "Youth": "The surrender of her weary ghost to the keeping of stars and sea was stirring like the sight of a glorious triumph" (Karl 267).

Next, a passage in verse from Algernon Charles Swinburne's "Nephelidia":

> Surely no spirit or sense of a soul that was soft to the
>   spirit and soul of our senses
> Sweetens the stress of surprising suspicion that sobs
>   in the semblance of sound and a sigh;
> Only this oracle opens Olympian, in mystical moods and
>   triangular tenses—
> "Life is the lust of the lamp for the light that is dark
>   till the dawn of the day when we die."
>
> (Grigson 219)

The description of one of the main characters in George Meredith's longish short story "The Case of General Ople and Lady Camper": "As for the men, they knew him to have faced the balls in bellowing battle-strife" (Karl 151). The context makes it obvious that "balls" refers to canon balls.

In Aristophanes's *Lysistrata* the old men of Athens ask themselves, "Tis ksullaboit an tou ksulou tōn Samō stratēgōn" (lit., Who will take with us of this wood among the generals at Samos?) (line 313). They mean something like, "Who among the generals at Samos is going to help us carry this wood?" and allude to the fact that the Athenian fleet has recently helped install a friendly regime in Samos. What concerns us here, though, is the repetition of the *ks* and *s* sounds. Two English translators have tried to reproduce the alliteration, but they have both had to change the sounds that carry it. One translation reads, "What general from the Samian lines an active hand will lend us?" in which the alliteration of the *l* is reinforced by the assonance of the *a* (Rogers 171). The other translation reads, "Oh, if they could bear a hand, those there seacaptains in Samos" (Way 16), relying mainly on the alliteration of *th* and *s*.

Allusion

Writers often allude to well-known texts in their own literature to give a sharper edge to the point they are making. Translators have to be able to recognize those allusions and to decide whether they should reproduce them in their translations. If they decide to do so and if they translate into a language that shares a culture with the language of the source text, their difficulties are minor. If they consider that an allusion in the original no longer enhances the writer's point, they may decide to replace it with another kind of allusion. In that case they are likely to face greater difficulties. If they are translating into a language that does not share a culture with the source language, they have to decide whether to introduce the allusion (and possibly explain it at some length in a footnote), to omit it, or to replace it by an allusion endemic to their own culture and analogous to the allusion found in the original. Biblical allusion could, conceivably, be replaced by Qur'anic or Buddhist allusions; allusions to the Greek and Roman classics could be replaced by allusions to the qasidahs, the *Manyoshu*, or the *Shih ching*, the early classics of Arabic, Japanese, and Chinese literature respectively. Translators have to decide whether this kind of strategy actually works. Four types of allusions are likely to occur with some regularity in literature written in English: biblical, classical, cultural, and literary.

Biblical Allusions

"Decency forbade that he should take the door off its rickety hinges, like Samson at the gates of Gaza" (Raffel 165). This allusion, taken from Rose Terry Cooke's short story "Grit," is to the biblical character of Samson, who took the gates of the Philistine city of Gaza off their hinges and carried them away. The allusion is made in the following context: Tom

Potter is in love with Phoebe, Reuben Fyler's daughter. When Reuben Fyler forbids him to see his daughter, Tom Potter gets angry. His first impulse is to "take the door off its rickety hinges," but he thinks better of it, not only because "decency forbade" it, but also because he is no Samson. The allusion, therefore, adds an ironic twist to the story.

Try to locate the referents of the biblical allusions below and discuss ways of rendering them in a translation.

The speaker in the following sentence is Dr. Jekyll in Robert Louis Stevenson's *The Strange Case of Dr. Jekyll and Mr. Hyde*: "The reversal of my previous experience seemed, like the Babylonian finger on the wall, to be spelling out the letters of my judgment" (Karl 236). To understand this allusion, translators have to read the Book of Daniel. Those who belong to a culture in which the Bible does not function as a central text may want to ask themselves whether there are better ways of rendering the allusion.

The following line of poetry is from the third canto of Alexander Pope's "The Rape of the Lock": Belinda, the heroine, starts a game of cards with the confident exclamation, "Let Spades be trumps! she said, and trumps they were" (Ewart 177). The tremendous irony of the allusion becomes clear when the line is read side by side with the beginning of the Book of Genesis.

The following stanza, from Thomas Love Peacock's "Rich and Poor, Saint and Sinner," alludes to two well-known phrases that occur in different parts of the Bible:

> The rich man's sins are hidden
> In the pomp of wealth and station;
>   And escape the sight
>   Of the children of light
> Who are wise in their generation.
> (Amis 53)

A biblical concordance is bound to shed light on this matter.

Classical Allusions

In "Bartleby the Scrivener," Herman Melville describes the main character, who lives in the Wall Street office where he works and accordingly also spends his Sundays there, as "a sort of innocent and transformed Marius brooding among the ruins of Carthage" (Raffel 106). The allusion is to the Roman general Marius, who lost the first civil war in the last century of the Roman Republic to his rival, Sulla. Marius retreated to the ruins of Carthage, which a victorious and then still united Rome had destroyed about half a century earlier, there to brood on the transience of things. Melville wants the reader to superimpose the desolation of Carthage on the desolate Wall Street of Bartleby's Sundays to heighten the impression of utter bleakness. He also takes care to call Bartleby an "innocent" Marius to establish the difference between his protagonist and the Roman general, who was guilty of the deaths of thousands of political opponents. Translators may want to ask themselves whether the allusion still works at a time when readers are less and less familiar with Greek and Roman history, both within Western civilization and without. They may want to think of acceptable analogies that might serve as substitutes. They may also want to consider whether it would be wise to use the same strategy in the examples listed below.

In *Don Juan* Byron refers to several scores

> Of those pedestrian Paphians who abound
> In decent London when the daylight's o'er.
> (Amis 65)

Translators need to find out what "Paphian" stands for, in either a standard dictionary or a dictionary of mythology, and decide whether to try to save the allusion or not—and how. Most translators will probably conclude that a straight calque of the word "Paphian" itself—simply transferring the root of the word to the target language and supplementing it with the morphological features appropriate in that language—will not be sufficient.

Samuel Butler alludes to a certain episode in the life of the Greek mythical hero Heracles in the last line of the stanza below, from "Hudibras." In the two preceding lines he alludes to other episodes from the hero's career. What are the three episodes, why are they alluded to, and what is to be done with them? Why is Heracles called a "hectoring hellcow" and why does he wear a lion's skin?

> Love's power's too great to be withstood
> By feeble human flesh and blood.

> 'Twas he that brought upon his knees
> The hectoring hell-cow Hercules;
> Reduced his leaguer-lion's skin
> To a petticoat, and made him spin.
>   (Amis 10)

In "The Case of General Ople and Lady Camper," George Meredith has the following comment on the hate letters Lady Camper keeps sending to General Ople: "Niobe under the shafts of Diana was hardly less violently and mortally assailed" (Karl 149).

Even in Aristophanes's *Lysistrata* there is a classical allusion; after all, Homer's texts had been recited, and later read, for centuries before Aristophanes was born. Half of line 520 reads "polemos d'andressi melēsei" (war concerns men). W. J. Hickie renders the allusion as "but war shall be a care to men" (414) and then adds a footnote, "facetiously adapted from the words of Hector to Andromache [Homer, *Iliad* 6.490]." Arthur S. Way eschews the footnote and tries to bring the allusion across in the text itself. He translates:

> Then he'd quote from the
> Homer he'd learnt at school, You
> Know, "War is man's sphere."
>   (25–26)

Cultural Allusions

Cultural allusions require from translators a more than superficial familiarity with the culture of which the source language is both the repository and the expression. When found lacking, that familiarity can be supplemented by encyclopedias. What encyclopedias fail to provide can usually be elicited from educated native speakers of the language. Over the years translators slowly compile their private encyclopedia of cultural allusions, based on their reading and their gradual further immersion in the source culture.

In his poem "Dora versus Rose" Austin Dobson uses the line, "From the tragic-est novels at Mudie's" (Amis 158). Mudie owned one of two influential lending libraries in Victorian England (W. H. Smith owned the other). People who could not afford to buy books got their reading matter from Mudie's or Smith's lending libraries. Most books supplied by those libraries would be the equivalents of today's best-sellers:

tearjerkingly tragic, sentimental, soon forgotten. They often told the story of a man torn between two women—precisely the kind of story Dobson parodies in his poem.

Further examples:

In his "Soliloquy of the Spanish Cloister," Robert Browning puts words in the mouth of the righteous monk, who detests his less righteous rival:

> I the Trinity illustrate,
>> Drinking watered orange-pulp—
> In three sips the Arian frustrate;
>> While he drains his at one gulp.
>>> (Amis 106)

Translators have to delve into early Christian theology to make sense of this allusion. They may decide that the allusion is too recondite to have meaning for the contemporary reader; they may also decide that at the same time it is an inalienable part of the poem's setting: Who but a monk would be able to speak in those terms? If they come to that conclusion, they will have to translate the passage as is and explain the allusion in a footnote. If they only think the allusion too obscure, they will have to cast about for alternatives.

In his poem "Annus Mirabilis," Philip Larkin describes the rapid change in sexual mores in England in the 1960s:

> Sexual intercourse began
> In nineteen sixty-three
> (Which was rather late for me)—
> Between the end of the Chatterley ban
> And the Beatles' first LP.
>> (Amis 314)

The Beatles are probably not yet a problem, but translators have to familiarize themselves with the publication history of D. H. Lawrence's *Lady Chatterley's Lover.* The "annus mirabilis" of the title, incidentally, represents both a cultural and a literary allusion. Translators should check dictionaries of classical antiquity as well as entries on that other English poet, John Dryden, in encyclopedias or in "companions" to English literature.

In "The Mark on the Wall," Virginia Woolf laments the fact that a woman's world is ruled and regulated by men. She decries the "masculine point of view which governs our lives, which sets the standard, which establishes Whitaker's Table of Precedency" (Karl 335). Translators have to find out what kind of book has "Whitaker" in the title and what the contents of that book are.

In *Lysistrata* 1092 Aristophanes writes, "ouk esth hopōs ou Kleisthenē binēsomen" (we shall have to make do with Kleisthenes). The line evokes a horrible vision of the future. If the men of Athens and the men of Sparta do not succeed in making peace, the women of all Greece will go on with their sex strike, and then the men will have to manage with Kleisthenes, a famous homosexual in Aristophanes's Athens. Benjamin Rogers leaves out the line altogether, not because he suddenly forgot all his Greek, but because he is operating on a hierarchically higher level of ideology: it is not "right" to talk about "such things." Douglass Parker tries to translate the allusion without having to resort to a footnote:

> It's Peace
> or we fall back on Kleisthenes
> And he's got a waiting list.
> (75)

Literary Allusions

Writers often allude to other works of the literature they are part of (or to works from other literatures) to make readers aware of similarities and differences between what they are reading and what is alluded to. The clash between the word on the page and the allusion evoked is designed to heighten the effect of the work.

In his poem "Beppo," Byron writes about the women of Venice:

> Their jealousy (if they are ever jealous)
> Is of a fair complexion altogether,
> Not like that sooty devil of Othello's
> Which smothers women in a bed of feather.
> (Amis 60)

The allusion is of course to Shakespeare's play *Othello*, in which the protagonist, a black man, kills his wife, Desdemona, a white woman, in a fit of jealous rage. Since there is a fair chance that Shakespeare's *Othello* is

known the world over, the allusion should not be too difficult to transfer
from source to target text. Translators who are members of African or
African American cultures might object to the allusion, though, and
might decide to replace it by one considered less offensive in their
cultures.

Further examples:

In "A Pindaric on the Grunting of a Hog," Samuel Wesley writes:

Freeborn Pindaric never does refuse
Either a lofty or a humble Muse:
Now in proud Sophoclean buskins sings
Of heroes and of kings.   (Amis 22)

Wesley exploits the clash between a lofty genre and a more trivial subject
matter. The question translators should ask themselves is whether this
clash still has any meaning for their potential audience. To be able to
answer that question, they should find out not just what a Pindaric ode
is but also what its status was among poets writing in England's Augustan age: whether it was a popular genre, widely practiced, or something more obscure and suspect. Translators also have to answer the
question why Sophocles is introduced and what buskins are.

Some allusions are used so often that they have become almost proverbial. Henry S. Leigh writes in his poem "Rhymes(?)":

My life—to Discontent a prey—
Is in the sere and yellow leaf.
(Amis 153)

The same allusion surfaces in Thomas Hardy's short story "The Three
Strangers," in which the baby whose christening directly or indirectly
brings all the main characters together is described in old age at the end
of the story, "[She] is a matron in the sere and yellow leaf" (Karl 185).
The source is again to be found in Shakespeare, but not in *Othello*.
Translators who are less familiar with Shakespeare may want to consult
a dictionary of quotations.

Line 563 of Aristophanes's *Lysistrata* reads, "heteros d'au Thraks
peltēn seiōn kakontion hōsper ho Tēreus" (another, like a Thracian,

shaking a small shield and a javelin like Tereus). The allusion is to a play by Aristophanes's "best enemy," Euripides. The play is called *Tereus*, and its eponymous hero is a Thracian indeed. To understand the allusion, the reader has to be familiar not only with the plays of Euripides that have been preserved but also with those plays of his that, like *Tereus*, have been lost. Present-day readers are unlikely to be familiar with either, but most translators of Aristophanes have not considered that fact. Donald Sutherland, for example, gives his readers the playwright, but not the play. He translates:

> a Thracian who, brandishing shield and spear
> like some savage Euripides staged once.   (22)

The anonymous translator(s) of *The Eleven Comedies* gives us the play, but not the author: "There was a Thracian warrior, too, who was brandishing his lance like Tereus in the play" (257). Most translators do not give their readers either, nor do they try to substitute any author or play likely to be better known to their readers.

Foreign Words

Foreign words within the body of a text to be translated raise the problem of double translation, or translation at one remove. Obviously the writer of the original put them there for a reason—an illocutionary reason. To "regularize" them, to translate them as if they were not foreign words in the original, may therefore be to detract from the complexity of the original. On the other hand, some foreign words (and phrases) may no longer sound foreign to the readers of the target language, in which case they will have lost the effect intended by the author. Translators have to decide for themselves. An expedient solution, used fairly often, is to leave the foreign word or phrase untranslated and then to append a translation between brackets or even to insert a translation into the body of the text a little later, where it would be expedient to do so. Obviously, this can be done much more easily in prose than in verse.

Sometimes, as in Arthur Hugh Clough's poem "Dipsychus," foreign words are used to add local color, and sometimes, as in the last line of the extract from that poem quoted here, they are used as euphemisms:

> The calm Madonna o'er your head
> Smiles, *col bambino,* on the bed

> Where—but your chaste ears I must spare—
> Where, as we said, *vous faites votre affaire.*
>
> (Ewart 317)

The Italian "col bambino" in connection with the "Madonna" of line 1 suggests a religious painting of the kind to be found, the author would have us believe, in many Venetian rooms used for the distinctly unholy purpose of prostitution. Painting and room are therefore at odds, and the "Madonna," but especially the innocent "bambino," heightens the contrast between background and action. It would probably not make much sense to leave the Italian phrase in a translation into Chinese or Arabic, both languages whose readers would, for the most part, not be as immediately arrested by the incongruity as would readers in Europe and the Americas.

The French "vous faites votre affaire" is an elegant way of saying "you do your thing," and the context makes it clear what kind of thing is meant. Besides serving as a euphemism by not sounding as crude as the expression in English, the French phrase in a Victorian English poem also signals a fairly acceptable way—faute de mieux—to talk about naughty things. Translators should ask themselves whether French plays the same part in the target culture they are translating for.

Further examples:

Anthony Thwaite's poem "A Girdle round the Earth" is an ironic reflection on the life and times of a British Council lecturer who moves from one country to another to teach English and, particularly, English literature. British Council offices do tend to "girdle" the globe, and the lecturer speaking in the poem looks back on his experiences in Japan:

> "King Rear was foorish man his girls make crazy"
> Says something certainly about the play.
> "Prutus falls on sord for bolitical reason"
> Is unambiguous, though not the way
> We native speakers might have put it . . .
>
> (Ewart 542)

The poet obviously quotes memorable lines from Japanese students' essays written in a course on "Saku Seppiya," or Shakespeare. In the first line the lack of phonological distinction between *r* and *l* in Japanese makes for an additional comic effect in the name "Lear." In the third line the poet similarly exploits the lack of phonological distinction between *p* and *b*. It might be very nice for a Japanese poet to put the shoe on the other foot and write a poem about the transmogrifications to which Western scholars subject Chikamatsu Monzaemon.

In Jean Rhys's short story "Mannequin," two models are engaged in a "conversation about the tristeness of a monsieur of their acquaintance" (Karl 404). The use of French in the English sentence suggests the degree of acculturation achieved by the story's English-speaking models living in Paris. The English suffix *ness* turns the French adjective *triste* into an almost English noun, and the English noun "acquaintance," of Romance origin, might almost be a French noun. Finally, "monsieur" is a word the English use when talking about the French.

In the anonymous medieval poem "Jolly Jankin," a girl is heard to say:

> Benedicamus Domino,
>   Christ from shame me shield!
> *Deo Gratias thereto—*
>   Alas I go with child!
> *Kyrie eleison.*   (Ewart 74)

The two Latin phrases and the one Greek phrase mixed in with the English are phrases an uneducated girl could have picked up from the Latin mass. They are most probably included in the poem to give the girl's prayer more weight: Christ might be more inclined to listen to someone who is able to pray—at least a little—in the language of the priests.

Genre

Genre is part of an inventory of literary devices shared by authors and readers alike. If poets entitle a poem "sonnet," they raise certain expectations in the reader's mind. Poets are then still free to go against these expectations, ironize them, parody them, and what not, but they can do so effectively only if readers know what to expect from a genre. Indeed, with the exception of the haiku, many non-Western genres have found it hard to be accepted in Western literature, simply because there is no obvious Western analog for the Arabic qasidah, for instance, or Chinese "rhyme-prose." Translators have to gauge to what extent their audiences are familiar with the expectations raised by the use of a genre and relied on by writers who make use of that genre. They have to develop strategies to match generic elements in the original accordingly.

The British poet Ted Pauker plays on the audience's generic expectations in a short poem called "Limeraiku," which combines the features of a Western genre, the limerick, with a Japanese genre, the haiku:

> There's a vile old man
> Of Japan who roars at whores:
> Where's your bloody fan.
> (Amis 291)

The first two lines are reminiscent of the first two lines of the limerick that usually set the scene. The whole poem is constructed on the typical haiku syllable sequence: five, seven, five. With the last line as is, the complete haiku resembles a truncated limerick. The poem is probably only translatable into cultures familiar with both genres.

Further examples:

Nathaniel Hawthorne uses a generic device recognizable as the Homeric simile in his short story "Young Goodman Brown":

> Thus sped the demoniac on his course, until, quivering among the trees, he saw a red light before him, as when the felled trunks and branches of a clearing have been set on fire, and throw up their lurid blaze against the sky, at the hour of midnight.   (Raffel 52–53)

The Homeric simile starts with the signal words *as when*. Called Homeric because it is often used in the *Iliad* and the *Odyssey*, the simile is introduced in those epics by the Greek equivalent of "as when" and can run on for as many as ten lines or more. Extended similes often function as a gloss on the main text or as a foil to it.

A. E. Housman's "Shades of Night" is constructed on the generic model of the ballad, as exemplified by the following extract:

> "Oh stay," the maiden said, "and rest
> (For the wind blows from the nor'ward)

Thy weary head upon my breast—
And please don't think I'm forward."
(Grigson 231)

The last line dips into another register and clashes with the rest of the extract, undermining the generic expectations confirmed by the first three lines. This effect would not be possible if the author and the readers did not share the generic expectations raised by the term *ballad*. It would also be hard, if not altogether impossible, to convey the subtle game of irony in cultures not familiar with the ballad. Translators could, of course, substitute a genre familiar to members of the target culture.

An untitled poem by Edward Lear plays on the genre of the gothic, or horror, story or verse tale:

The lone Yaourt sails slowly down
The deep and craggy dell—
And from his lofty nest loud screams
The white plumed Asphodel.
(Grigson 107)

The setting is immediately recognizable for aficionados of the genre. If the genre is not widely known in the target culture, no amount of skill on the translators' part can make the translation a success in that culture.

Catullus's second poem is a parody of a hymn to a god or goddess. Lesbia's sparrow becomes like a divine being to Catullus since the bird is so close to Lesbia all the time. The first three lines of the poem, quoted here, follow the traditional structure of the hymn: they consist of a series of appositions listing the attributes of the godhead.

Passer, deliciae meae puellae,
quicum ludere, quem in sinu tenere,
cui primum digitum dare appententi. . . .
(1–3)

(Sparrow, darling of my girl
with whom to play, whom in her bosom to hold,
to whom desiring to give the tip of her finger. . . .)

Only two of the translators of Catullus mentioned in the Works Cited list for this chapter tried to achieve a similar effect through the use of similar pragmatic means. George P. Goold translates:

> O sparrow that are my sweetheart's pet,
> with whom she likes to play, whom to hold in her lap,
> to whose pecking to offer her finger tips.   (33)

The "O" reinforces the idea of the invocation. The concatenation of appositions, often straining the syntax of the English language, serves the same purpose. Barriss Mills translates:

> Sparrow, my sweetheart's pet,
> whom she likes to play with, and holds
> in her lap, and offers her fingertip.
>   (24)

He tries for the hymn effect but shies away from too severe a dislocation of English syntax and may fail to get across the mock ritual as a result.

Finally, a freebie to reiterate a point. Although genres are part of the inventory of literary devices, they are by no means limited to literature. The following is the complete "text" of Edward Lear's "A Letter to Evelyn Baring":

> Thrippsy pillivinx,
>   Inky tinky pobbleboskle abblesquabs?—
> Flosky! beebul trimble flosky!—Okul
> scratchabibblebongibo, viddle squibble tog-a-tog,
> ferrymoyassity amsky flamsky ramsky damsky
> crocklefether squiggs.
>   Flinkywisty pomm,
>   Slushypipp.   (Grigson 107)

Obviously the information content of the poem is not excessive. In fact, Lear is merely filling with nonsense words the "canonized," socially accepted form of the genre called "letter," the better to draw attention to the features of the genre: the salutation, set apart typographically and followed by a comma; the question, probably inquiring about the addressee's health and well-being; the exclamation of delight at the anticipated answer; the actual news to be told; the final greetings, again set apart typographically and again followed by a comma; the name of the sender, also set apart. Translators have to replace Lear's nonsense with nonsense that looks acceptable in the target language. If the socially accepted form of the letter is different in the target culture, they have to make some adaptations.

Grammatical Norms

Writers sometimes deviate from the accepted grammatical usage of their time, not because they are incapable of writing well, but because they wish to focus attention on their "mistake." Translators should try to match the grammatical error in the source language with a grammatical error in the target language if they consider the error of sufficient importance within the framework of the overall composition of the source text.

In his poem "Little Billee," William Makepeace Thackeray has the following two lines:

> Says gorging Jim to guzzling Jacky
> We have no wittles, so we must eat we.
> (Amis 101)

The right grammatical usage would of course replace the final "we" by something like "ourselves." But "ourselves" would upset the meter and lose the rhyme. Moreover, the final "we" fits in well with the somewhat uncouth language of the three sailors in the poem. The "wittles" in the last line, which should really read something like "victuals," reinforces that impression.

Further examples:

In O. Henry's short story "One Thousand Dollars," Miss Lauriere's "mistaken" use of the personal pronoun in the objective case alerts the reader to the comparative rank Mr. Gillian occupies in her esteem: "[H]er dresser mentioned the name of Mr. Gillian. 'Let it in,' said Miss Lauriere" (Raffel 442).

The mistake should be easy to reduplicate in other Indo-European languages but difficult to render in languages that do not differentiate personal pronouns according to gender.

In "Sharing Eve's Apple," John Keats plays on the noun "blush" as representing a much more abstract concept and keeps up the play by applying it to the modals "won't" and "shan't," the nouns "thought" and "naught" linked by assonance, and the past participles "done" and "begun."

> There's a blush for won't and a blush for shan't
> And a blush for having done it:
> There's a blush for thought and a blush for naught,
> And a blush for just begun it.   (Ewart 253)

At least part of the effect of the poem is achieved by this circumvention of abstract moral concepts, which puts the whole passage on a footing of levity. Restoring such concepts in a translation would reduce the effect. To do without abstract moral concepts, translators may have to change the grammatical categories by which the original makes its points: verbs may have to be turned into nouns and vice versa. Translators may often have to recur to shifts in grammatical categories to safeguard the tone of the originals, that is, to safeguard the originals' illocutionary power.

Writers frequently shift grammatical categories to intensify the illocutionary power of their texts. Witness the following lines taken from John Gay's *Beggars' Opera*:

> All professions be-rogue one another.
> The priest calls the lawyers a cheat;
> The lawyer be-knaves the divine.
>   (Ewart 163–64)

The prefix "be" turns the nouns "rogue" and "knave" into verbs meaning "turning into" a rogue or a knave. The process should not be hard to reproduce in languages with analogous morphological systems. It might be more difficult in languages lacking that system.

In "Things," D. H. Lawrence does violence to English syntax to express the urgency of the yearning of the vine:

> [T]here is a certain waving of loose ends upon the air, like the waving, yearning tendrils of the vine that spread and rotate, seeking something to clutch, something up which to climb towards the necessary sun.   (Karl 347)

Translators have to decide what to do with the syntax of the target language.

In Aristophanes's *Lysistrata* the Spartan messenger identifies himself as follows: "Karuks egōn, ō kursanie, nai tō siō / emolon apo Spartas peri tan diallagan" (I am a herald, oh young whippersnapper, by the gods, I have come from Sparta for the reconciliation) (983–84). The messenger speaks the Doric variety of classical Greek, in which Athenian *e* sounds become *a* sounds and Athenian *theō* (gods, in this case the twin gods Castor and Pollux, associated with Sparta in mythology) becomes "siō." In *Aikin Mata*, a translation-transposition of Aristophanes's play for a Nigerian audience, T. W. Harrison and J. Simmons make the Spartan messenger a member of the Nigerian Yoruba tribe, and they render his lines in pidgin: "Ah ben wan talk say ah come for talk of peace" (63).

Metaphor

At the end of Stevenson's *Dr. Jekyll and Mr. Hyde,* Dr. Jekyll refers in his written confession to "the animal within me licking the chops of memory" (Karl 239). There is no real animal inside Dr. Jekyll, nor does memory have anything like "chops." But once we are prepared to admit that there is a figurative animal inside Dr. Jekyll, that animal is given the characteristics of all other animals, including chops and the right to lick them. These chops can then be connected with memory.

What we observe at work here is metaphorization. Concepts that do not normally belong together are linked in such a way as to increase the illocutionary power of the passage, preferably without overly straining the reader's credulity or sense of propriety. Translators will find that their readers' sense of propriety tends to act as a check on the translation of metaphor: collocations of concepts or words that do not unduly strain one culture's concept of what is acceptable (logically, emotionally, even morally) may be found beyond the pale of the acceptable by members of another culture. Translators may have to adapt or substitute accordingly, but they should do so only as a last resort since one characteristic of metaphor is that it requires some flexibility of mind to be understood and that it can impart a similar flexibility on the target language. Since flexibility is always a good thing, translators might do well to consider the potential benefits of the "unacceptable" before rejecting it.

Because metaphors tend to be short, I list more examples under this heading than I have under previous headings. Students have to find out the literal meaning of the two concepts, try to explain how they enter into the bond of metaphor, and then try to explain why certain of these metaphors are translatable, and how, whereas others might not be.

In "Who Was She?" Bayard Taylor refers to "spindle-shanked youths" (Raffel 160), bonding a part of the body with a part of a machine.

In John Dos Passos's "Great Lady on a White Horse," a girl talks to the protagonist from behind the door she has just opened and keeps ajar. She apologizes for her behavior, not in a sentence she herself utters, but in a sentence presented as either the protagonist's observation or the narrator's interjection: "A smile coyly bridged the crack in the door" (Raffel 463). The story begins with a sentence, printed in italics, designed to anchor the whole tale on a certain level of experience: "Morning clatters with the first L train down Allen Street" (Raffel 462). To understand the bonding of the concepts in this metaphor, translators have to find out what an "L train" is. Some may then decide that the metaphor is too far fetched (too distinctly modern) to be salvaged in certain cultures.

In Dylan Thomas's "One Warm Saturday," the hero is running down the beach, trying to catch a ball and "tripping over a castle into a coil of wet girls" (Karl 477). The word "coil" is normally not used to describe a group of girls but rather a certain type of animal. The use of the word here not only increases the power of the passage but also foreshadows the protagonist's experience with a particular girl at the end of the story.

Line 928 of Aristophanes's *Lysistrata* reads, "All hē to peos tod Heraklēs ksenizetai" (But this penis here, it's Heracles regaled). The rather humorous context needs to be explained before the reader can appreciate the line. The line is spoken by an Athenian soldier who has come home on leave and wants to sleep with his wife. The wife, however, has sworn Lysistrata's oath, and she will not break off her sex strike for him. She therefore leads him on, telling him to wait while she goes and gets another pillow, some more perfume, anything. Finally, she disappears and leaves him in the lurch.

The allusion to Heracles would have been immediately obvious to the audience. Known to be a voracious eater, Heracles was often teased by his hosts, who would let him wait long periods before they would put food on the table. The analogy between Heracles's situation and that of the homecoming soldier should be clear but that does not make the line any easier to translate. Dudley Fitts tries the rather obvious "I don't suppose even Herakles / would stand for this" (81), in which the pun on "stand" is easily deflated. Jack Lindsay offers a somewhat cerebral circumlocution that will probably be lost on an audience unfamiliar with mythological lore: "They treat you just like Heracles at a feast / With cheats of dainties" (89–90). Only Parker finds a—to my mind at least—perfectly acceptable modern analogue, without any recourse to the cerebral or the discursive: "What a lovefeast! Only the table gets laid!" (66)

Names

Writers sometimes use names not just to name characters in a poem, story, novel, or play but also to describe those characters. The name usually contains an allusion to a certain word in the language, and that allusion allows readers to characterize characters to a greater extent than names like Smith would—or Brown, the name of the protagonist in Hawthorne's "Young Goodman Brown" (Raffel 45–57). Brown itself is a neutral name, but Goodman, which originally meant something like "mister" and is no longer in current usage, tends to add a positive shade of meaning, precisely—ironically—because it is no longer current. Other names in the story are more obviously allusive or even symbolic. Brown's wife is called Faith, whereas a woman reputed to be a witch is called Cloyse, a name that has overtones of "insipid" or even "distasteful." The deacon, on the other hand, is called Gookin. But in the story things are not necessarily what they seem, and bad characters can have good names. The writer uses the discrepancy between the character as revealed in the story and the name of that character to create irony.

Further examples:

"Miss Asphyxia" (Raffel 125–35), the title of a short story by Harriet Beecher Stowe, aptly describes its protagonist.

In Hamlin Garland's "Return," one of the old women in the village is referred to as "Mit' Snidely" (Raffel 207). The artist's model of a rather low class in Henry James's "The Real Thing," who turns out to be flexible in many ways but never really likable, is called Miss Churm (Raffel 233), evoking a combination (a mental metaphor?) of a kind of animal and a grinding motion.

Writers can also give characters neutral names and then proceed to characterize them anyway, with cultural allusions linked to those names through wordplay. A character in Dos Passos's "Great Lady on a White Horse" is a man called Oglethorpe. When asked what he is like, another character in the story responds jokingly, "Oh, did the Ogle come out of his lair?" (Raffel 466). By mentioning "Ogle" and "lair" in the same sentence, the author creates a cultural allusion that makes the reader see Mr. Oglethorpe in a particular way. By putting the allusion in the mouth of another character, the author also hedges his bets: what the character thinks about Mr. Oglethorpe may be borne out by the rest of the story, or it may not. Readers have to react accordingly.

It is also possible to make literary allusions on the basis of names, and many writers do so. In his poem "The Journal of Society," Godfrey Turner has one character ask another, "Oh, have you seen the *Tattlesnake* and have you read what's in it?" The *Tatler* was the name of a famous eighteenth-century English journal, edited by Joseph Addison and Richard Steele and influential in the development of the essay as a genre in England. Later the name was taken over by many other journals, usually devoted less to the development of worthy literary genres than to the simpler joys of gossip, mild to mean. The second part of the journal title referred to (or invented) in this poem gives the reader sufficient grounds for suspecting the nature of the gossip printed in it.

Line 397 of Aristophanes's *Lysistrata* reads, "ho theoisin echthros kai miaros Cholozugēs" (the enemy to the gods and the defiled one, Cholozuges). The reference is to a generally known, but not generally liked, demagogue of the time. Alan Sommerstein translates, "the damnable scoundrel" (196), and adds in a footnote, "In the Greek *Cholozuges,* a name compounded of *cholos* (anger) and Demostratus' nickname Buzyges" (250). Things get a little complicated here: the character's real name is the rather innocuous Demostratus. His nickname is Buzyges, and his nickname in the play is Cholozuges. Other translators try to render the Greek double entendre in the text, without recourse to footnotes. Way, for example, translates, "Young Pick-a-quarrel" (20), obviously referring to the *cholos* in Cholozuges. Lindsay calls the character a "lunatic ox" (48), going back to his nickname in real life: the "Bu" in Buzyges is linked to the noun *bous,* meaning "ox." Arthur Wheelwright does nothing at all to the name: he merely transliterates it and writes, "that wretch Cholozyges" (78). The reader who does not know Greek probably does not even suspect that wit has been attempted in the original, especially since Wheelwright does not take the trouble to append a footnote. Perhaps the most "baroque" translation is Sutherland's. He writes, "that god-Damn-ox-tratus" (16), keeping the general sound pattern of Demostratus, the character's real name, adding "god" to "Damn" to make doubly sure the audience gets the hint about Aristophanes's feelings toward the character, putting in the "ox" that refers to Demostratus's nickname, and adding the "tratus" for local color. It is not easy to decide which of the solutions proposed is the best one. Nor is it necessary to do so: they merely serve as examples that can inspire other translators or warn them away from a possible course of action.

Neologisms

Sometimes writers invent new words to strengthen the illocutionary power of their texts. Just as all that is new builds on something already in place, these new words are variations on existing words or combinations of parts of existing words. Translators have to decide how important a given neologism is and whether they can build analogous neologisms in their own languages or achieve analogous illocutionary effects some other way.

In "Wigs and Beards," Robert Graves begins a line with the word "Moreunder," adding "(which is to subtract, not add)" (Amis 232). It is easy to see which word "moreunder" is a variation on, and it can probably be translated accordingly.

Further examples:

In "A Grouchy Good Night to the Academic Year," Ted Pauker describes the vice-chancellor of a university cajoling the great of the land "[a]t influence-dinner or grovel-tea" (Amis 285). Translators need to know that here "tea" means much more than a bag, or even loose tea. Once they understand this, they can easily understand "grovel" and "influence," particularly if they are the least bit familiar with academic funding.

In Dos Passos's "Great Lady on a White Horse," a character is described as having "a sharp fragillycut nose" (Raffel 471). The nose seems to be almost equated with an item of clothing, which is also "cut" in a certain way.

In "The Case of General Ople and Lady Camper," George Meredith says of the female protagonist, "All semblance of harshness and harridan-like spike-tonguedness vanished when she said adieu" (Karl 137). It is not difficult to identify the hidden simile in "spike-tonguedness." Not all languages may be able to build a formal analogy, but all may have ways of conveying an analogous simile.

The eighth line of Catullus's second poem reads, "sit soliaculum sui doloris" (may it [the sparrow] be a small solace to her pain). The word "soliaculum" is a neologism invented by Catullus. Some translators try to render it by a neologism of their own, or at least an attempted one, whereas others translate it "straight," thereby depriving the audience of one of the features for which the original was prized in its time. William Hull may indulge in too many words when he renders Catullus's one line by two of his own: "She finds a pain in miniature / and defined a precise relief" (4). Peter Whigham comes perhaps closest to the original with his "a little solace for her satiety" (8). Theodore Martin seems to prefer cliché to neologism in "finding balm" (5). James Michie opts for the relatively banal "relief" (19), and Mills is satisfied with the equally banal "respite" (24). Carl Sesar tries to render the neologism by morphosyntactic, rather than morphological, means; he translates, "things to soothe the pain a little." Finally, J. H. A. Tremenheere falls for the Victorian cliché of the Roman man-woman relationship. He translates, "pretty follies such as these" (39).

Off-Rhyme

Howard Moss's poem "Tourists" contains the following two lines:

> Finding in Frankfurt that one indigestible
> Comestible makes them too ill for the festival.
> (Ewart 518)

"Indigestible" does not rhyme with "festival" in the strict sense of the word; in fact, the sound sequences underlying both words are so dissimilar that they exclude the very idea of rhyme. They are near rhymes, or off-rhymes, and they are very difficult to translate, not the least because off-rhymes frequently pair words from two different linguistic registers (or two spheres of experience as they are expressed in language) to achieve a comic or ironic effect. Translators have to decide whether off-rhyme plays a part in their own poetics comparable to the part it plays in English. If it does, they should be tempted to reproduce it. If not, they can no doubt achieve comic or ironic effects in other ways.

Further examples:

The clash between registers is obvious in the following stanza taken from P. G. Wodehouse's poem "The Gourmet's Love Song":

> Around me myriad waiters flit,
>> With meat and drink to ply men;
> Alone, disconsolate, I sit,
>> And feed on thoughts of Hymen.
>> (Amis 213)

The somewhat mercenary, or at least money-oriented, attitude implied by "ply men" contrasts sharply with the speaker's elevated thoughts of marriage referred to here by its archaic Augustan name, "Hymen."

A similar clash occurs in Browning's "The Pied Piper of Hamelin," in the passage where the Piper addresses the rulers of the city:

> You hope, because you're old and obese,
> To find in the furry civic robe ease?
>> (Ewart 303)

The clash is heightened by the unusual syntactic pattern in the second line.

In "Peekaboo, I Almost See You," Ogden Nash suggests that his readers should own two pairs of glasses:

> One for reading Earle Stanley Gardner's Perry
>> Mason and Keats's "Endymion" with,
> And the other for walking around without saying
>> Hallo to strange wymion with.
>> (Ewart 450–51)

The off-rhyme between "Perry" and "saying" is, to put it mildly, not all that easy to savor, but the opposition "Endymion-wymion" involves both off-rhyme and neologism. On another level, the pairing of Perry Mason and Endymion could be interpreted as a "conceptual" off-rhyme in its own right. Again, translators have to ask themselves what kind of "name recognition" "Earle Stanley Gardner's Perry Mason" and "Keats's 'Endymion' " are likely to get in the target cultures. Translators have to translate accordingly.

Lindsay uses off-rhyme in his translation of lines 677–78 in Aristophanes's *Lysistrata,* mainly to render the implied comparison of two situations much more explicit. Perhaps he goes too far, but that is for the reader to decide. Aristophanes writes, "hippikōtaton gar esti chrēma kapochon gunē / kouk an apolisthoi trechonotos" (a woman is a very horse-friendly thing, not prone to falling off at all; she does not even slip off when the horse gallops). Lindsay translates:

> For everyone knows how talented they all are in the saddle,
>> Having long practiced how to straddle;
> No matter how they're jogged up and down,
>> They're never thrown.   (69)

Parody

Of all works of literature, the one that is written to make fun of another is probably the most difficult for translators because they find themselves translating not just one work but two, the parody and the original. Since without the original, the parody loses most, if not all, of its raison d'être, the translation of parody requires alertness to the work(s) parodied. The successful translation of parody is, however, largely out of the translator's hands. A parody is successfully translated only if readers in the target culture find it funny. If they are to be amused, they must, unfortunately, have a rather wide knowledge of the source literature. To say that that is usually too much to expect is not to criticize the members of the target culture: many members of the source culture who are not interested in its literature cannot enjoy the parody either. They may discard it as "boring," or, more charitably, they may comment that "it must be nice if you know the original." Parody, then, is where the translator's impotence stands most glaringly exposed, through no fault of his or her own.

Translators who try to translate a parody into a certain language before its original has been translated probably set themselves an impossible task. Yet this situation sometimes arises, simply because the need, the demand, or just the sheer desire to translate does not always respect the chronological evolution of the source literature. When trying to translate a parody, translators might be well advised to focus on a work in the target literature that could be said to occupy a position roughly analogous to the one occupied by the work parodied in the source literature. They could then substitute allusions ad hoc or even wholesale. Unfortunately, the work of literature they focus on in the target culture should be relatively well known in that culture; otherwise the parody will fail to amuse more than the literary few. If no analogous work in the target literature can be found, the translator has little choice but to indulge in extensive use of footnotes, which might work up to a point, but nearly always stamps the translation as "scholarly" and thus keeps it away from the wider audience the translator may have had in mind while translating. Ideally a translator might try to translate the original and the parody at the same time.

A further complication arises when the work to be translated—*Don Quixote*, for instance—parodies not just a particular work but a whole genre. Such a parody may have some advantages for translators if it is to be translated into literatures sharing the same wider culture. If *Don Quixote* is to be translated into the literatures of Europe and the Americas, many of which possess romances of chivalry, the target readers are likely to be familiar with the genre being parodied. If, however, *Don Quixote* were to be translated into a literature outside that wider culture, the point of the parody would probably be lost, even if the work of the translator were of the highest illocutionary power. Translations of genre parodies into another culture tend to reach only those readers who are already familiar with the source literature. They do not need the translation in the first place or are likely to use it as a convenient crib, demoting it to a text that "refers" to the source text rather than fully "represents" it. Yet parodies are immensely important in the evolution of a literature: they usually signal the awakening of a school, group, or individuals willing and able to attack the poetics and the ideology of the dominant school, group, or individuals. But since the evolution of literature is mainly studied by scholars and not by ordinary readers, translations of parodies appreciated by scholars may be the best translators can hope for.

When Byron writes in *Don Juan*, "The world is all before me—or behind" (Amis 70), the first two-thirds of that line parodies the fourth-to-last line of Milton's *Paradise Lost*:

> The world was all before them, where to choose
> Their place of rest, and providence their guide.

Milton's lines express optimism in the future of humankind: even though Adam and Eve have been expelled from Paradise, they can now start a new life on earth. Byron's narrator—a persona very like Byron— is much less convinced of either humanity's rosy future or his own. Hence the ironic undermining of the first part of the line by "—or behind."

Further examples:

In the following extract from "Wordsworth Unvisited," Hartley Coleridge parodies a contemporary of Byron's:

> Unread his works—his "Milk White Doe"
>   With dust is dark and dim;
> It's still in Longman's shop, and oh!
>   The difference to him!   (Amis 72)

The first line contains half of the title of one of William Wordsworth's less successful longer narrative poems, and the last line—except for the last word—repeats a famous line from a shorter Wordsworth poem. Translators have to make use of collected editions or dictionaries of quotations to find out precisely what is being parodied. They also have to find out what "Longman's shop" was and why it is important in this context.

G. K. Chesterton's "After Walt Whitman" does not parody a particular line or work of Whitman's; rather, it caricatures that poet's style, described as "Whitmanian catalog" by his admirers and in more disparaging terms by his detractors. The best possible translation of this poem will mean little to readers not familiar with Whitman:

> Me clairvoyant
> Me conscious of you, old camarado,
> Needing no telescope, lorgnette, field-glass, opera-glass, myopic
>   pince-nez,
> Me piercing two thousand years with eye naked and not
>   ashamed;
> The crown cannot hide you from me;
> Musty old feudal-heraldic trappings cannot hide you from me.
>   (Amis 203)

The parody sounds some well-known Whitmanian themes: the poet as seer, the poet as a friend (camarado) to all men, and the poet as champion of liberty in both present and past.

Anthony Brode's "Breakfast with Gerard Manley Hopkins" parodies the style of another poet, a near contemporary of Whitman's. Hopkins is perhaps most remembered in the evolution of English poetry for his so-called sprung rhythm. By departing from the practice of his peers and predecessors and counting stresses in a different way, more reminiscent of Anglo-Saxon poetry (as was his heavy use of alliteration), Hopkins tried to "loosen" or "free" the metrical constraints of poetry that he felt were stifling creativity. The effect sprung rhythm had on contemporary readers was underwhelming. Most of them dismissed it as "strange" or worse. Contemporary students of English poetry still find Hopkins hard to read, but sprung rhythm has been accepted as a standard device in English poetry. Nobody writes sprung rhythm anymore, however. The parodist quoted below has been reminded of sprung rhythm by—of all texts—the advertisement printed on the box of cereal he tried for breakfast:

> "Delicious heart-of-the-corn, fresh-from-the-oven flakes are sparkled and spangled with sugar for a can't-be-resisted-flavour"
> —*Legend on a packet of breakfast cereal.*

Serious over my cereals I broke one breakfast my fast
    With something-to-read-searching retinas retained by print on
    a packet;
Sprung rhythm sprang, and I found (the mind fact-mining at
    last)
An influence Father Hopkins fathered on the copy-writing
    racket.   (Amis 315)

The poem is unlikely to go over well with the general reader in cultures where breakfast does not entail eating cereals out of boxes or where Hopkins is virtually unknown, unless members of those cultures are aware, or can be made aware, of Anglo-American breakfast habits and unless the poetry written in those cultures can boast a figure analogous to Hopkins.

Aristophanes did not like Euripides at all. Consequently, he parodies him wherever he can, most obviously in *The Frogs* but also in *Lysistrata.* Lines 706–07 read, "Anassa pragous kai bouleumatos, / ti moi skuthrōpos ekselēluthas domōn?" (Mistress of our deeds and our wishes / why do you come out of the house with a sullen look?). Their comic effect is heightened in the original when the "Mistress," Lysistrata, the leader of the sex strike, appears looking sullen because certain women have been discovered breaking the strike. Euripides's high-flown style therefore clashes with the actual situation in which the lines are spoken. Benjamin Rogers tries to achieve a parodistic effect by simply overdoing the diction of his translation. He writes, "Illustrious leader of this bold emprize / What brings thee forth, with trouble in thine eyes?" (190). The "emprize" and the "brings thee forth" should alert readers to the fact that a different register is being used, even though they may not always, or even usually, know why.

Patrick Dickinson ignores the problem altogether and, probably in the interest of readability, simply translates:

> Lady, why so gloomy? What's the matter?
> You, the leader of our glorious . . . .
> (103)

The most ingenious solution has been proposed by Alan Sommerstein, who makes use of the by now "quaint"-sounding diction of Victorian translations of Euripides (of the kind ridiculed by T. S. Eliot in his well-known "Euripides and Mr. Murray" article) to create a "generic" parody, in which the reader does not really have to know who precisely is being parodied. Sommerstein writes:

> Lady who did this daring plot invent,
> Why from thy fortress com'st thou grim-looked out?
> (210)

The elision is a hallmark of Victorian translations of the Greek tragedians, as is the compound "grim-looked" and the syntax, which is impossibly contorted for no immediately obvious reason. The following example gives the reader another taste of Victorian "translationese" and the opportunities it afforded for parody.

A translation is written in translationese if it can be immediately identified as a translation, and not a very good one: it looks awkward and sounds unnatural in the target language. There may be reasons to produce this kind of translation, and I discuss them in chapter 3. For the time being we merely need to know that the poet and classical scholar A. E. Housman was less than charmed by the strange translationese used for Greek tragedies by his contemporaries and predecessors. He parodied that translationese (producing, in effect, a parody to the sec-

ond power) in his "Fragment of a Greek Tragedy." I quote some of the
lines spoken by the Chorus:

> O suitably-attired in leather boots
> Head of a traveller, wherefore seeking whom
> Whence by what way how purposed art thou come
> To this well-nightingaled vicinity?
> My object in enquiring is to know
> But if you happen to be deaf and dumb
> And do not understand a word I say,
> Then wave your hand, to signify as much.
>
> (Amis 176–77)

Housman particularly parodies the slavish imitation of Greek syntax. In
classical Greek the noun in the vocative can be preceded by a whole
string of adjectives, here "suitably-attired in leather boots." "Head of" is
a Greek way of referring to a person. At the very beginning of Sophocles's *Antigone*, the protagonist addresses her sister Ismene as—in a
translation into the translationese Housman parodies—"O dear own-
sibling head of Ismene," which simply means something like "My dear
sister Ismene." The second half of the second line and the whole third
line parody the facility with which classical Greek can string question
words together. "Well-nightingaled" parodies the translations of the
Greek "epitheton ornans," the adjective usually found together with, or
bound to, a noun, as in "fleet-footed Achilles," to give another example
in Housmanese. The last four lines no longer parody the slavish adher-
ence to Greek syntax but, rather, imitate the often pedestrian language
the leader of the chorus uses to address the protagonists of the drama.

Poetic Diction

A style of writing is apt to be called poetic when it exhibits a fairly dense
concentration of illocutionary power in relatively few words, stanzas, or
paragraphs. It was long thought that such a concentration of illocutionary power is possible only in poetry. To prove that it is also possible in
prose, I quote only prose passages in what follows. On the level of technique, poetic diction is perfectly translatable. Whether it succeeds with
the target audience depends largely on whether the poetics dominating
the target literature at the time a translation is made sets great store by
poetic diction.

We find the following passage in Garland's "Return":

Morning dawned at last, slowly, with a pale yellow dome of light rising silently above the bluffs, which stand like some huge storm-devastated castle, just east of the city. (Raffel 195)

Alliteration is one hallmark of poetic diction, as are hallowed words, or, rather, words often bound to other words and always identified as belonging to a more elevated level of language use. "Morning," for instance, hardly ever "breaks" in poetic diction; it always "dawns." Translators should be able to identify these hallowed words, or word pairs, and to reproduce them on the same elevated level of language use in the target language. Alternatively, though, if translators feel the poetic climate in their own literature is not very receptive to poetic diction, they may want to tone it down. They may be convinced that the original has other features that are likely to appeal to the target audience and that might be needlessly obscured by the use of poetic diction on a matching level of intensity.

Further examples:

In the short story "A New England Nun" Mary E. Wilkins Freeman describes a road as follows: The road was bespread with a beautiful shifting dapple of silver and shadow; the air was full of mysterious sweetness. (Raffel 217)

Again, mark the alliterations. Poetic diction also operates on the morphological level: it tends to build new words by using affixes (prefixes, suffixes, and infixes) normally no longer productive on other levels of the language, like the prefix "be" in "bespread." Another word identified as belonging to the level of poetic diction would be "dappled"—a word that, incidentally, was a favorite of Gerard Manley Hopkins's.

In Edith Wharton's "A Journey," the protagonist, traveling by train with her sick husband, realizes at some point in the journey that her husband is dead:

[S]he felt a sudden prolonged vibration, a series of hard shocks, and then another plunge into darkness: the darkness of death this time—a black whirlwind on which they were both spinning like leaves, in wild uncoiling spirals, with millions and millions of the dead. . . . (Raffel 354)

Once more, note the alliterations. In poetic diction death is often associated with darkness and a whirlwind that blows men and women away like leaves. Leaves do not turn, but "spin." Similarly, spirals nearly always "coil" or, of course, "uncoil."

Jack London describes the canyon of the title of his short story "All Gold Canyon" as follows:

> But the air was sharp and thin. It was as starlight transmuted into atmosphere, shot through and warmed by sunshine, and flower-drenched with sweetness. (Raffel 399)

Alliteration, to be sure. Poetic diction also makes use of latinate, "learned" words like "transmuted." In poetic diction the air is often "drenched with" some scent or other, almost never "pervaded by" or some such equivalent.

Poetic diction can carry a translator rather far from the original, as is evidenced by Lawrence Housman's translation of lines 964–66 of the *Lysistrata* as, "I am borne upon a flood / Of rage and love and longing" (64). The original reads as follows: "Poios gar (et) an nephros antischa / poia psuchē, poisi d'orcheis / poia d'osphus" (What kidneys can resist this / what soul, what testicles / what loins?). Housman's poetic diction is meant to detract from the "baseness" of the original. His translation of *Lysistrata* becomes more understandable if the reader is told that it was written for, and produced by, the theater of the suffragette movement in England before World War I. Way stays on middle ground with his "Through night after night condemned to burn / And to have no sport when the dawns return" (43), which ironizes the diction of Romantic love poetry without stumbling into the anatomical. Again, Sommerstein is the most original translator, exploiting the clash of registers in the original both to use poetic diction and to ironize it in his translation, "What heart, what soul, what bullocks could long endure this plight?" (220).

Pun

A pun is a play on two of the meanings a word can have. Because readers must make a conscious effort to distinguish between the different meanings of the word and to find out which one the author intended, the pun activates two meanings at the same time. Readers get both the obvious usual meaning of a word *and* the frequently less obvious, more unusual meaning the author intended. They get the "norm" and the "deviation" from that norm simultaneously. The clash between the two heightens the pun's illocutionary power.

It is easy to see where problems arise in the translation of puns. Consider the following example, taken from Samuel Beckett's short story "Yellow": "Belacqua cut the surgeon" (Karl 464). Belacqua, the main character in the story, is scheduled to undergo surgery for the removal of a toe. He is not thrilled by the prospect and tries to cheer himself up with mental exercises in black humor. When he finally gets to the operating room, he "cuts" the surgeon. The culturally determined pattern of expectation readers have developed to deal with this type of situation (based on movies, other books, accounts by people who have had surgery) calls for exactly the opposite: the surgeon is supposed to cut (into) Belacqua.

It may take readers a few seconds to realize that Beckett uses the verb "cut" in the sense of "ignored, gave the cold shoulder to." The clash between the obvious expected sense of "cut" and the sense in which it is used here heightens the illocutionary power of the sentence. The pun on "cut" can be translated successfully only if the target language has a word or phrase that means at the same time "make an incision" and "ignore." If the target language does not have such a word or phrase, the pun may be irretrievably lost.

But translators often retrieve puns in another way: if they lose a pun in one passage, they will often try to gain one in another. Translators frequently insert puns of their own to make up for puns they found themselves unable to translate. Since the pun turns out to be an important stylistic feature of the source text, it is probably advisable to keep the number of puns in source text and translation roughly the same. Since, moreover, a pun that is not translated as a pun still yields its information content and since a pun that is translated where there was no pun in the original only heightens the illocutionary power of the passage without notably changing the information content, no real harm is done by the insertion of "new" puns.

If a target language cannot reproduce both the meanings suggested by the word "cut" in the source text, translators can still use the target language's word for "ignore" and communicate the necessary information. If they hit on a "punnable" word or expression later on, they simply add the illocutionary power of the additional pun to the information content, which is not impaired in any way.

Further examples:

In Thomas Hood's poem "Faithless Sally Brown," the pun is made possible by one additional letter that shows up in the printed version of the punnable word but is not heard when that word is pronounced:

> They went and told the old sexton, and
> The sexton toll'd the bell.   (Amis 78)

Students should establish the meanings of "told" and "toll'd" and try to find a word or phrase in the target language that can match them.

Another "faithless" woman addresses her lover, who has just come home a cripple from the wars, in the following lines from the same poet's "Faithless Nelly Gray":

> "Why then," said she, "you've lost the feet
>   Of legs in war's alarms,
> And now you cannot wear your shoes
>   Upon your feats of arms!"   (Amis 79)

The pun based on the formal analogy between "feet" and "feats" both establishes that the lover has had his legs amputated and indicates the questionable practical value of heroic deeds.

In Collin Ellis's "The New Vicar of Bray," the pun is based on the alternation between the noun "life" and the cognate gerund of the verb *to live,* namely, "living," which takes on a specific meaning within the clerical context of the passage:

> When I took orders, war and strife
>   Filled parsons with misgiving
> For none knew who might lose his life
>   Or who might lose his living.
>   (Amis 227)

This example can serve as a warning to translators against "punnitis," a rather common deformation of the critical sense caused by continued overexposure to literary texts. Punnitis causes translators to discover puns where none were, most probably, intended. It would be possible, for instance, to discover a pun on "orders" in the stanza quoted above. The original "Vicar of Bray," described in an anonymous eighteenth-century poem with the same title, is a notorious turncoat always ready to follow all kinds of different orders, no matter how contradictory they may be. His twentieth-century successor, the "New Vicar of Bray," shares this trait with his eighteenth-century eponym. Accordingly, we may assume that he, too, delights in following orders. The information conveyed by "following orders" can, of course, also be expressed by the phrase "to take orders." That phrase has a very distinct meaning in clerical language, namely, to become a cleric. "When I took orders" in the first line might therefore be (construed as) a pun.

Readers who find the above, if not totally implausible, at least pretty farfetched are absolutely right. The example documents the extent to which punnitis can lead translators astray. Punnitis also shows up in authors, at times, and manifests itself in so-called bad puns. Bad puns are bad because they are too obvious, and, rather than heighten the illocutionary power of the passage, they insult the reader's intelligence, as in the following example from Stevenson's *Dr. Jekyll and Mr. Hyde*: " 'If he be Mr. Hyde,' he had thought, 'I shall be Mr. Seek' " (Karl 195). The reference to the game of hide-and-seek is a bit too facile for intellectual comfort.

Near the beginning of Aristophanes's *Lysistrata* the heroine, Lysistrata, and her friend, Kleonike, meet with a delegate from Sparta, who has come to express the Spartan women's interest in the proposed sex strike designed to bring an end to the war. As they look at the—naked—Boeotian woman, Lysistrata and Kleonike indulge in the following dialogue:

> LYSISTRATA: Nē Di hôs Boiōtia / kalon g'echousa to pedion
> KLEONIKE: kompsotata tēn blēchōn ge paratetilomenē
> $$(87-90)$$
>
> (LYSISTRATA: By Zeus, a Boeotian, and she has a beautiful plain.
> KLEONIKE: The pennyroyal has been torn out of it very well
> indeed.)

In Greek antiquity the plains of Boeotia were proverbial for their beauty, but Lysistrata is clearly referring to another kind of "plain," namely, one that should cover the Boeotian woman's groin but does not, since Greek women took great care to epilate that part of the body in an effort to make themselves more attractive to men. Kleonike follows Lysistrata's train of thought by referring to the process of epilation, linking the Boeotian woman's pubic hair with the pennyroyal, a weed. Both have been "torn out."

Some translators choose to ignore the pun altogether, though not necessarily because they think they will not be able to match it or at least find an equivalent. Housman, who, as mentioned, translated *Lysistrata* for the suffragette theater in England, feels that the pun would demean the very heroines he is supposed to glorify. Accordingly, he refuses to translate it and merely shifts the Boeotian woman's hair from one part of her body to another. His translation of Aristophanes's pun reads, "O fair Boeotia, with the full sweet breast / And locks wherein the sunlight seems to rest" (11). The "sunlight," it should be noted, "rests" nowhere in Aristophanes. In the translation it serves both to ennoble the Boeotian woman and to fill out the meter of the second line.

Other translators choose to translate simply "as is" and hope that the audience will catch the pun. This strategy is followed by, among others, the anonymous translator(s) of *The Eleven Comedies*, where the lines quoted above read as follows: "Ah! my pretty Boeotian friend, you are as blooming as a garden / Yes, on my word, and the garden is so prettily weeded too" (232).

Finally, translators rely on the gestural context to make the pun more obvious for those readers or spectators who might otherwise miss it. In this way they add another dimension to the verbal pun, turning it into a situational pun or a pun to the second power. Parker uses that approach in his translation of the Lysistrata-Kleonike dialogue:

LYSISTRATA: *As they inspect Ismenia* Ah, picturesque Boiotia: her verdant meadow, her fruited plain. . . .
KLEONIKE: *Peering more closely* Her sunken garden where no grass grows.
A cultivated country. (13)

American readers are also supposed to recognize the cultural allusion in the "fruited plain."

The following is another example of a pun to the second power, an exclusively verbal one, this time, but one that also relies on the judicious use of euphemism. It is taken from the anonymous "Susannah and the Elders":

Susannah the fair
With her beauties all bare
Was bathing her, was bathing herself in an arbor,
The Elders stood peeping and pleas'd

With the dipping
Would fain have steered into her harbour.
(Ewart 195)

The pun is constructed around the similarity between "arbor" and "harbour." It is also understood that "harbour" is not to be taken literally, as a place where ships sail to and from, but rather as a euphemism for a certain part of Susannah's anatomy. The use of this kind of euphemism—usually in a sexual or erotic context—is sometimes referred to by the French phrase *double entendre,* literally, "double understanding." Needless to say, the effectiveness of this combination of pun and double entendre is further predicated on the audience's ability to decipher the biblical allusion in the source text.

Puns can also be made on the basis of the differences and similarities between the "common" language all members of a linguistic community speak and understand and the much more specialized language, often referred to as jargon, spoken and readily understood by members of a given profession but not by speakers outside that profession.

The following example is taken from Lewis Carroll's "The Palace of Humbug":

The well-remembered voice he knew,
He smiled, he faintly muttered: "Sue!"
(Her very name was legal too).
(Grigson 101)

Puns can also be predicated on cultural allusions, which may make them even more untranslatable. Consider the following example from Walter de la Mare's poem "Archery":

The luck must hold; the child stand still:
This William befell;
But just how close was core to corse
Could only William tell.
(Grigson 258)

The solution of the riddle lies in the last two words of the last line: "William tell." If we change the typography slightly (puns can also be based on typographical alterations), we get "William Tell." By looking up that name in an encyclopedia or a historical dictionary or even a history of Switzerland, we can come up with a context in which it becomes obvious why "the luck must hold" and why "the child must stand still." Students infected by punnitis can further speculate about "core"—the part of the apple that plays a prominent part (with apologies) in the story of Wilhelm Tell—and "corse," an archaic spelling for "corpse" used here as one more typographical trick.

There are also false puns, in which the meaning of the pun word intended by an author is so far removed from the obvious meaning that readers have to think hard before they even discover that the obvious meaning is not the intended one. They usually reach that conclusion because the obvious meaning is, on reflection, seen not to fit the rest of the text.

The following passage from Meredith's "The Case of General Ople and Lady Camper" makes things clearer:

> He [the general] had killed the soft ones, who came to him, at-tracted by the softness in him, to be killed; but clever women alarmed and paralyzed him.   (Karl 118)

Readers exposed to just this passage may be forgiven for thinking that the general is some kind of Bluebeard. Readers who have read the whole story know that the general is far too kind even to think of impersonating Bluebeard. The "killing" referred to must therefore be taken to mean the gentlemanly art of lady-killing.

A similar, though perhaps slightly overobvious, example can be found in the following passage from Hardy's short story "The Three Strangers": "The most salient of the shepherd's domestic erections was an empty sty at the forward corner of his hedgeless garden" (Karl 170). The mind boggles at what readers infected with punnitis and blessed with a rudimentary knowledge of the works of Sigmund Freud might do with words like "salient," not to mention phrases like "empty sty" and "hedgeless garden."

Finally, puns can also be based on literary allusions. In another example from Beckett's "Yellow," we find the following conversation between Belacqua, the protagonist about to lose a toe to surgery, and a Scottish nurse: " 'Such a lang tootsy' she giggled. . . . 'Soon to be syne' he said" (Karl 461). Because the nurse is Scottish, she says "lang" instead of "long." She also uses "tootsy" as a term of endearment for "little toe." To figure out the rest of the riddle, students should refer to the collected works of the Scottish poet Robert Burns.

Register

Except in grammar books or primers on style, language is never used in a vacuum: it is always used in a certain situation. In different cultures a specific use of language is considered appropriate (or inappropriate) in a specific situation. If you are introduced to the queen of England, for instance, greeting her with a boisterously enthusiastic "Hi, Queen" is sure to get you in trouble with the chief of protocol, perhaps even lead to your being quietly escorted from the premises. An appropriate use of language in this situation would be a humbly mumbled "Your Majesty." Moreover, you are not to start talking to her effusively about the weather back home; rather, in calm and measured tones, she will ask you who you are; you will tell her who you are, also in calm and measured tones; she will thank you for the information, turn away, and, in all likelihood, promptly forget it.

Writers can exploit all kinds of discrepancies between utterance (the use of language) and situation (the particular context in which language is used) to heighten the illocutionary power of their texts. In what follows, we shall look at various strategies. Translators have to make sure that the registers, the types of utterance felt appropriate to a given situation, are similar, or at least analogous in different cultures. If they are not, the illocutionary power of the source text will not be heightened by a mere literal translation of the words on the page in what amounts to a cultural vacuum. As in dealing with puns, translators would be wise to ascertain how important register is as an illocutionary feature of the source text and to try to keep the incidence of register-based illocutionary items roughly identical in source and target texts. If they cannot translate specific register-based illocutionary items, they may have to compensate by adding register-based illocutionary items where the target culture would allow such an addition.

Utterance and Situation

In *Don Juan,* Byron describes women hunting for men as follows:

> Though several also keep their perpendicular
> Like poplars, with good principles for roots;
> Yet many have a method more *reticular—*
> "Fishers for men," like sirens with soft lutes.
> (Amis 68)

The "hunting for men" situation, usually motivated by erotic or pecuniary considerations, or both, and not infrequently comical, is dignified here by the use of two latinate words: "perpendicular" and "reticular," which conjure up connotations of a scientific, or at least "learned," use of language. A closer look at the dictionary reveals that _perpendicular_ merely means "standing upright." The word therefore suggests that some women, presumably the ones with "good principles," do not stoop to assuming nonperpendicular positions in this kind of situation and that others, who use the "more reticular" method, might not be disinclined to do so. "Reticular" means "pertaining to a little net" and indicates that these women are actively fishing—almost in the literal sense of the word. Further elaborating on the semipun suggested by "reticular" are two allusions in the last line. One is biblical: in the New Testament Christ tells his apostles to be "fishers of men"—not "for" men, which is Byron's ironic twist. The other allusion is classical: the sirens were seductive female mythical creatures who used music to lure sailors from their ships and to their deaths by drowning.

Further examples:

In his poem "Dover to Munich," C. S. Calverley describes the breaking of his pipe in a register that is much too high for the actual occurrence. The register could be appropriate for epic writing or, more likely, as is hinted in the passage, for Shakespearean tragedy, but it is not appropriate for the discovery of a broken pipe. The discrepancy between utterance and situation once again creates a comic illocutionary effect:

> Ah! why starts each eyeball from its socket,
>   As, in Hamlet, start the guilty Queen's?
> There, deep-hid in its accustomed pocket,
>   Lay my sole pipe, smashed to smithereens!
> (Amis 123)

Sometimes a character in a story sits in judgment over the register used by another character, as in Meredith's "The Case of General Ople and Lady Camper." Lady Camper objects to some of General Ople's expressions, and he gradually stops using them. The three words proscribed by Lady Camper are "gentlemanly," "bijou," and "thanks," all of which she deems "vulgar" or at least not in keeping with the general's situation in life. The following extract shows the general trying to match his personal utterances to his personal situation as defined by Lady Camper:

> [A] gent—a residence you would call fit for a gentleman. I call it a
> bi [Pause] it is, in short, a gem. . . . Tha [pause] I thank you very
> much.   (Karl 149)

Sometimes writers play on the discrepancy between utterance and
situation in another manner. By writing a certain line (such as the first
line in the following passage from John Betjeman's "Westminster Abbey"), they awaken certain expectations in their readers—here the expectation of an "elevated" register suited to a description of the nation's
principles. They then proceed to undermine those expectations totally
or in part. Betjeman produces this effect by writing down a judicious
mixture of the elevated and the less elevated that, besides being comic,
reveals a rather insular frame of mind:

> Think of what our Nation stands for;
>   Books from Boots and country lanes,
> Free speech, free passes, class distinction,
>   Democracy and proper drains.
>   (Amis 250)

The effect is further heightened by the juxtaposition of positive ("de-
mocracy") and negative ("class distinction") elements; they are mentioned in the same breath in a matter-of-fact tone that blurs the positive-
negative distinction and creates the impression that "this" is not just
"how things are" but also how they are meant to be.

Situation and Situation

Writers can also heighten illocutionary power by juxtaposing two situations (each with its attendant utterance, or "right" register) that are not
usually juxtaposed. The juxtaposition of the literary and the culinary in
Hood's "To Minerva" is an example:

> So, Thyrsis, take the Midnight Oil,
>   And pour it on a lobster salad.
>   (Amis 80)

The first line contains two allusions to classical literature. "Thyrsis" is a
name commonly encountered in the pastoral poetry of antiquity, and
the "midnight oil" also evokes a time when one could study late at night
only by the light of oil lamps. The second line could have been lifted
from a cookbook. Each utterance is appropriate to a certain situation,

but the situations are not normally juxtaposed in such a flagrant manner. Hence the comic effect.

In his parodistic poem "The Sorrows of Werther," Thackeray juxtaposes basically the same situations to the same effect, but his stanza is predicated exclusively on the reader's familiarity with a specific work of literature: Goethe's novel *The Sorrows of Young Werther.* It had been a cult novel all over Europe not too many years before Thackeray wrote the following lines:

> Werther had a love for Charlotte
>   Such as words can never utter;
> Would you know how he first met her?
>   She was cutting bread and butter.
> (Amis 102)

Needless to say, the assonance, or half rhyme, in the second line, which serves as a bridge between the two situations juxtaposed, also heightens the comic effect.

Charles Dickens also juxtaposes two situations not normally juxtaposed when he describes the villain in his short story "Hunted Down":

> His hair, which was elaborately brushed and oiled, was parted straight up the middle; and he presented this parting to the clerk, exactly (to my thinking) as if he had said, in so many words: "You must take me, if you please, my friend, just as I show myself. Come straight up here; follow the gravel path; keep off the grass; I allow no trespassing."
> (Karl 31)

Utterance, Situation, and Time

Sometimes, especially in writing about the past, writers try to re-create a certain "historical register," an utterance that would once have been appropriate to a given situation. Here is Hawthorne, in "Young Goodman Brown":

> [P]rithee put off your journey until sunrise and sleep in your own bed tonight. A lone woman is troubled with such dreams and such thoughts that she's afeard of herself sometimes. Pray, tarry with me this night, dear husband.
> (Raffel 46)

These are the words Faith uses to try to make her husband, the protagonist, stay home for the night and begin his journey the next morning. People no longer spoke like that in Hawthorne's time, but the author must have felt that an attempt to re-create the register of Puritan New England as he imagined it would lend greater authenticity to his story. In re-creating registers of the past, writers also play with time. The narrator uses the language of Hawthorne's day, and the characters use the language Hawthorne re-created for them. One can easily imagine this kind of historical register being used for parodistic purposes as well.

If writers play with time, the reverse is also true. Sometimes words change their meanings or at least their connotations with the passage of time and through no fault of the author. As a result, the reader does not at first read a certain word in the sense the author intended it. When Conrad says of a character in his short story "Youth," "Mahon . . . unexpectedly developed all a Frenchman's genius for preparing nice little messes" (Karl 253), he does not mean that what Mahon has prepared needs to be cleaned up; he means that it needs to be eaten. Translators must either quietly regularize the usage here and undo what time has wrought or else use a word in their own languages that has become archaic in the same manner—which might be hard to find.

Time has played a similar prank on the word "die" in the following extract from John Dryden's "Song of Marriage-à-la-Mode":

> The Youth, though in haste,
> And breathing his last,
> In pity dy'd slowly, while she dy'd more fast;
> Till at length she cry'd, Now my dear, now let us go,
> Now die, my Alexis, and I will die too.   (Ewart 120)

Students have to consult the *Oxford English Dictionary* or an etymological dictionary of the English language to find out one of the connotations the verb *die* had in Dryden's time and has lost since. That connotation puts a whole different slant on the passage.

Finally, consider how time has affected one single word in a sentence fragment from Hawthorne's "Young Goodman Brown"—ironically, a sentence in which the author is not trying to re-create any historical register. Rather, the narrator merely reports what the protagonist perceives: "the minister and Deacon Gookin, jogging along quietly" (Raffel 51).

False Friends

Certain registers of language tend to become specialized—sometimes to such an extent that the ordinary user of language who is not familiar with a given register and therefore tends to interpret the word on the page in its nonspecialized sense is likely to misread the author's intention. Once again, translators may have to quietly regularize if words or registers in the source language do not match those of the target language.

When Poole, Dr. Jekyll's butler, "stamped on the flags of the corridor" (Karl 190), in Stevenson's *Dr. Jekyll and Mr. Hyde,* he is not actually stamping on pieces of cloth imbued with a strong symbolic value.

Similarly, when the narrator of Conrad's "Youth" says, "When the ship was fast we went to tea" (Karl 248), he does not mean that the ship is traveling at top speed while the characters in the story are daintily sipping the celebrated brew from fine china cups.

In London's "All Gold Canyon" the protagonist is prospecting for gold. The method he uses is described as follows: "With a quick flirt he sent the water sluicing across the bottom, turning the grains of black sand over and over" (Raffel 402). In this context the word "flirt" does not mean what it means to most speakers of English today. Students may have to go to *Webster's* for enlightenment.

Jargon

Different professions are notorious for using highly specialized registers of the language. Translators have to find out what the words or phrases mean, usually in a monolingual dictionary, and then go hunting for equivalents in a bilingual dictionary. Since some of the professions that occupy analogous positions in various societies (such as law, for instance) are generally heavily marked by the historical evolutions of those societies, the target language may well have no exact equivalents available, forcing translators once more to quietly regularize. It is in fact notoriously difficult to translate "accurately" into English any legal term from any European country that has a code of law based on the old *Code napoléon,* because the code of law in England and in its historical dependencies is rather different.

Consider the use of nautical jargon in the following passage from Conrad's "Youth":

> And while we pumped the ship was going from us piecemeal: the bulwarks went, the stanchions were torn out, the ventilators smashed, the cabin door burst in. (Karl 250)

To translate passages like this one, translators may have to recur to pictorial dictionaries that have labeled illustrations of whatever is portrayed.

In Liam O'Flaherty's "The Touch," men are gathering seaweed on a beach described as follows: "Now there were many cocks of the red weed scattered over the gray sand" (Karl 407). Translators have to find out what "cocks" are in this context and then look for a suitable equivalent in their own language. The equivalent may be harder to find in languages spoken in landlocked countries than, for instance, in Japanese.

In "The Gold Bug," Edgar Allan Poe introduces a character as "an old negro, called Jupiter, who had been manumitted" (Raffel 59). "Manumitted" is dated legal jargon, and writers writing today would probably use another verb.

Sociolect

The use of a certain sociolect identifies members of the same social group. When people move from one social group to another, the register they use is likely to change.

Hardy gives a good illustration of the process in his poem "The Ruined Maid." The following stanza renders a conversation between two girls who were once members of the same rural social group. The girl who has moved to the city has had to pay in a nonlinguistic manner for her incorporation into a new social group that sanctions her use of a new sociolect:

> —"At home in the barton you said 'thee' and 'thou,'
> And 'think oon' and 'theas oon,' and 't'other'; but now
> Your talking quite fits'ee for high compa-ny!"
> "Some polish is gained with one's ruin," said she.
> (Amis 160)

Since the country-city opposition is fairly common in all cultures, translators should not find it too difficult to come up with the requisite analogs in their target languages.

The following conversation between the narrator and the old black servant in Poe's "The Gold Bug" illustrates the clash between two sociolects. In fact, the two sociolects in question are so different that the old servant at first does not understand what the narrator has just said to him:

> "Well, Jup, perhaps you are right: but to what fortunate circumstance am I to attribute the honor of a visit from you to-day?"
> "What de matter, massa?"
> "Did you bring any message from Mr. Legrand?"
> "No, massa, I bring dis here pissel."   (Raffel 64)

When the narrator realizes that the servant does not understand him, he "moderates" his sociolect. Even then, communication is not perfect. The servant's sociolect uses the word "pissel" (a variant of *epistle*) to refer to what the narrator's sociolect calls "message."

Time tends to date sociolects rather quickly. The last word of the phrase to be quoted from E. M. Forster's "The Story of a Panic" must have been part of the sociolect of a certain social group at the time the story was written. It is now no longer used in that sense by members of that group: "[W]alking was such a fag" (Karl 311).

In Aristophanes's *Lysistrata* the Spartans speak their own, Dorian, variant of Greek, which appears to the Athenians as a funny kind of sociolect. When the Spartan envoy comes to Athens to discuss peace at the end of the play, the following interchange takes place between the leader of the Athenian council and the Spartan messenger:

> PRUTANIS: All estukas, ō miarōtate
> KERUX: Ou ton Di' ouk egōga mēd' aupladdiē
> (989–90)
>
> (LEADER: But you have an erection, o most defiled one.
> HERALD: No, by Zeus, not me, don't talk nonsense.)

The leader of the council has mistaken the Herald's staff (which turns out to have other uses as well, as we shall see) for a more biological-anatomical phenomenon, hence his opening line to the Spartan. It is interesting to see how translators have used nearly all variants of register described here to try to render the dialogue. The most obvious strategy is to merely replace one sociolect by another that is perceived to play a similar part in the receiving culture. The two perennial candidates for this kind of sociolect switch are Scots and something perhaps best defined as "Generic Southern American," as used by Sutherland, for example: "But you have an erection, you reprobate!" "Bah Zeus, Ah've no sech thing! And don't you fool around" (37). "Reprobate" is an example of the use of jargon: it is not unlikely that the leader of the council, who drafts legal documents, would resort to this term.

Sommerstein's Spartan speaks Scots. His translation reads as follows: "Why, you rascal, you've got prickitis!" "No, I hanna. Dinna be stupid" (221). The word "prickitis" is used, in addition, to mock the jargon of the medical profession.

The anonymous translator(s) of *The Eleven Comedies* play(s) on the discrepancy between utterance and situation in: "Ah, ha! my fine lad, why I can see it standing, oh fie!" "I tell you no! but enough of this foolery" (279). "Lad" and "standing" are used to convey the notion of "erection," and yet the translation remains polite and polished enough for a Victorian audience (albeit one consisting of "private subscribers") to enjoy, precisely because utterance does not match situation.

Way's translation gives us an example of the relation between utterance, situation, and time. It reads, "O you scamp, / It's stiff." "Not it, by Jove, don't talk such rot!" (44). Both "scamp" and "rot" are more than a little dated now. They also both point to the speaker's sociolect: he must belong to the upper class (at least as suggested by the English text) and "have a way with rascals," possibly because he has "done a few rascally turns" himself, "in his time," of course.

Finally, Patrick Dickinson fuses the utterance-situation relation and "false friends" into a felicitous pun. He translates, "Are you stiff from your journey?" "The man's nuts" (114). The word "stiff" is plausible within the context of the situation, except for the fact that the stiffness has not been caused by traveling. By combining the two meanings of "stiff," Dickinson also manages to convey the erection, reinforcing the effect in the reader's mind by the use of the other false friend—potential pun contained in the word "nuts."

Idiolect

The notion of idiolect is perhaps best explained by the following extract from Stephen Crane's "The Blue Hotel":

> Scully's speech was always a combination of Irish brogue and
> idiom, Western twang and idiom, and scraps of curiously formal
> diction taken from the storybooks and newspapers. He now hurled
> a strange mass of language at the head of his son. "What do I keep?
> What do I keep? What do I keep?" he demanded in a voice of thun-
> der. He slapped his knee impressively, to indicate that he himself
> was going to make reply, and that all should heed. "I keep a hotel,"
> he shouted. "A hotel, do you mind? A guest under my roof has sa-
> cred privileges. He is to be intimidated by none. Not one word shall
> he hear that would prejudice him in." (Raffel 328)

The solemnity of the occasion forces Scully, the owner of a hotel in a
small town, to have recourse to formal diction in the third and fourth
sentences of his reply to his own question. But the formal diction is su-
perseded by a combination of brogue, twang, and idiom in the second
and last sentences of that reply.

Idiolect, as opposed to sociolect, refers to the personal register, the
individualized use each speaker makes of a language. But since each
speaker is also a member of at least one social group belonging to the
larger group of all users of that language, the distinction between idiolect and sociolect is not always easy to make and even less easy to maintain. Translators should be able to recognize that both present problems
and ideally to solve those problems. They should not waste their time
trying to decide whether a certain problem is more likely to be caused by
idiolect than by sociolect or vice versa.

The speaker in W. H. Auden's "Uncle Henry," for instance, pro-
nounces the *r* in a way that used to be characteristic of the sociolect of a
certain upper-class group in England between the wars. The poem also
makes clear that Uncle Henry has certain sexual preferences. Whether
they affect his idiolect or not is a moot question and had better remain
so. A more fruitful question is whether Uncle Henry's oddities in sociolect (and idiolect?) can be reproduced in other cultures. It is extremely
unlikely that translators can reproduce these oddities by using the same
phonetic feature, but they may have analogous features from all levels of
language at their disposal. This is what Uncle Henry has to say:

> Weady for some fun,
>   visit yearly Wome, Damascus,
> in Mowocco look for fwesh a-
>   -musin' places.

> Where I'll find a fwend,
> don't you know, a charmin' cweature,
> like a Gweek God and devoted:
>   how delicious!   (Amis 258)

Accents are probably the phonological features that most clearly identify an idiolect. Listen to the German accent in C. G. Leland's "Hans Breitman's Barty":

> Ve all cot troonk ash bigs.
> I poot mine mout' to a parrel of beer
>   Und emptied it oop mit a schwigs
> Und den I gissed Matilda Yane
>   Und she shlog me on de kop,
> Und de gompany vighted mit daple-lecks
>   Dill de coonshtable made oos shtop.
>   (Amis 110)

The phonological features are obvious: w is pronounced v, g is pronounced k, p is pronounced b, and f is pronounced v. Furthermore, s followed immediately by a consonant is pronounced sh. Some prepositions are used in a "creative" way in English, and some German words are sprinkled in. The idiolect or, more likely, the combination of sociolect and idiolect implies some kind of value-laden commentary on Hans Breitman and his peers. Translators have to isolate a group of people held in analogous disesteem by members of the target culture and play with features of that group's sociolect.

Finally, here is an idiolectal feast, taken from Cooke's "Grit." Reuben, the protagonist, has lived in the same village all his life. He breaks his leg but decides to continue home in his horse cart. On the way he meets an Irishman. They indulge in the following masterly dialogue:

> "Say, have you got a jackknife?" was Reuben's salutation.
> "Yes, surr, I have that; and a fuss-rate knoife as iver ye see. What's wanting?"
> "Will yer old hoss stan'a spell?"
> "Sure he'll stand still the day after niver, av I'd let him. It's standin' he takes to far more than goin'!"
> "Then you git out, will ye, 'nd fetch yer knife over here 'nd cut my boot-leg down."

"What 'n the wurrld are ye after havin' yer boot cut for?" queried the Irishman, clambering down to the ground.   (Raffel 167)

Language Variants

In his "Ballad of Abbreviations," Chesterton says of an American businessman:

> And he yells for what he calls the Elevator
> A slang abbreviation for a lift.
>
> (Amis 204)

The lines are construed around a basic fact of language development: that the same language, spoken in a different environment, will develop in different ways. Sometimes, though not necessarily, value judgments may be attached to these ways.

In William Faulkner's "Turnabout," two British sailors have been playing their own private game of "beaver," the word they use for "basket mast." When they mention the game to two American friends they have just made, the Americans interpret it quite differently at first since "beaver" has a specific slang meaning in American English. In fact, Faulkner exploits rather than creates a "transatlantic" pun that is the result of the separate development of two variants of the same original language. Translators into relatively homogeneous languages, where similar developments have not occurred, may therefore find it difficult to reproduce this kind of pun unless they use dialect variants of their target languages. The passage reads as follows:

> [The British sailor says,] "No beaver then. Had me two down a fortnight yesterday."
> The Americans glanced at one another. "No beaver?"
> "We play it. With basket masts you see. See a basket mast. Beaver! One up."   (Raffel 523)

Burns wrote his poems in another variant of English. Translators have to judge whether it is feasible, or worthwhile, to try to reproduce the particular flavor of the original. Whatever variant of their own languages they use to take the place of Scots is likely to sound artificial and may even make the translation less intelligible. The variant may, moreover, awaken connotations among target-language readers that differ vastly from the connotations readers of English usually attach to Scots. In addition, "flavored" translations that deviate significantly from dominant linguistic norms may be dismissed as "incorrect."

The "flavor" argument seems to lose its force the farther one goes back in time. Once the language variant becomes a historical variant, a previous stage of the same language, the flavor ceases to matter. Nobody would argue that Shakespeare should be translated into sixteenth-century German, for instance, or François Villon into fifteenth-century English, even though Dante has been translated into mock-thirteenth-century French and mock-thirteenth-century German.

Here, in any case, is a stanza from "Tam o' Shanter." Students should determine the meaning first and then discuss possible strategies for reproducing the illocutionary effect achieved by the use of Scots.

> Weel mounted on his gray mare, Meg,
> A better never lifted leg;
> Tam skelpit on thro dub and mire,
> Despising wind, and rain, and fire;
> Whiles holding fast his gude blue bonnet;
> Whiles crooning o'er some auld Scots sonnet.
> (Ewart 212)

Students may have to go to a Scots dictionary or use the convenient shortcut of an annotated edition of the complete Burns.

Rhyme and Meter

Rhyme—identical stressed vowels and the consonants succeeding them at the end of a word—has been the hallmark of Western poetry for about fifteen hundred years, sometimes becoming the identifying feature of poetry as such: what did not rhyme was not poetry. During those years, poetry was also produced according to certain meters.

Rhyme is difficult to translate into language with a different vowel and consonant distribution. Meters are not easily transposed from one language to another, certainly not from an Indo-European language to a non-Indo-European language and vice versa. Non-Western cultures do not always use end rhyme in their poetry, even though virtually all known poetry is constructed around some kind of sound similarity or sound repetition and some kind of rhythm, which may or may not be regulated into formal meter.

Translators who translate with rhyme and meter as their first priority often find themselves neglecting other features of the original: syntax tends to suffer most as it is stretched on the procrustean bed of sound similarity and metrical beat, and the information content is almost inevitably supplemented or altered in none too subtle ways by "padding": words not in the original added to balance a line on the metrical level or to supply the all-important rhyme word. Poets and translators have been very much aware of this device; witness the following lines from Carroll's "A Quotation from Shakespeare with Slight Improvements":

P. This sleep is sound indeed, this is a sleep
    That from this golden rigol hath divorced
    So many English—
K.   What meaneth "rigol," Henry?
P. My liege, I know not, save that it doth enter
    Most apt into the metre.
K.   True, it doth.

                                        (Grigson 97)

Although the arguments against translating poetry into rhymed and metered verse are persuasive, rhyme can play an important part in the original poem: it marks a completion, a rounding of the line, and acts as a further "marker" in the development of the poem as a whole. Furthermore, the sound effects produced by the succession of rhymes undoubtedly heighten the illocutionary power of the poem, especially in some genres of poetry.

In practice, translators have to decide whether a poem would be fatally weakened if the rhyme was taken out of it. Rhyme can be said not to add much to a fair number of poems beyond providing a certain deadening, or at least soporific, regularity. Translators have to weigh the advantages and disadvantages of producing a rhymed and metered target text. Does the use of rhyme and meter militate against other important components of the poem: syntactic elegance, balance, and economy of information?

Translators also have to take into account the role played by meter and rhyme in the poetics that currently dominates the target literature. Does it set great store by rhyme and meter, or is free verse in favor? Would producing a rhymed and metered translation of a certain poet irretrievably date him or her in the target literature because the dominant poetics does not emphasize rhyme or meter? Alternatively, if the dominant poetics does consider rhyme and meter important, is it receptive to "foreign" patterns of rhyme and meter or does it insist on its own? Can a sonnet, for instance, be effectively translated as a sonnet into a given non-Western literature, or does it have to be adapted to an indigenous pattern of rhyme and meter?

Perhaps the most trivial, but also most basic, guideline to be observed is this: Do not produce a rhymed and metered translation if you are not totally confident you can do it well. If an unrhymed and unmetered translation of a rhymed and metered poem reads well, the translator has done a greater service to the author of the original than he would have by producing a rhymed and metered translation very obviously identifiable as such. Also, do not insist on imposing a pattern of rhyme and meter that is likely to alienate prospective readers in the target culture. The production of translations can be used as a weapon in the struggle for domination between two types of poetics. The Chinese modernist poet Feng Chi deliberately and consciously translated Western sonnets in the sonnet form—which is by no means indigenous to classical Chinese poetics—to further the cause of an alternative, nonclassical poetics. I have more to say about this and similar aspects of translation as they influence the development of literatures in chapter 4.

An example of an original in which rhyme does not play a vital part and might therefore conceivably be left out in translation is the following. A character in Dos Passos's short story "Great Lady on a White Horse" is composing a poem in her head as she rides the bus. Initially, however, she produces little more than strings of likely rhyme words to pick from:

> When thou and I my love shall come to part, Then shall I press an ineffable last kiss Upon your lips and go . . . heart, start, who art . . . bliss, this, miss. . . . (Raffel 469)

Exposing the mechanism of composition also exposes the rather mechanical nature of the rhyming that, it could be argued, adds nothing of great illocutionary power to the poem about to come into being.

Translators may be tempted to render the same verdict on the rhyme in the last line of the following extract from Byron's "Beppo" or if they take both rhyme and meter into account, even on the passage as a whole:

For dance, and song, and serenade, and ball,
    And masque, and mime, and mystery, and more
Than I have time to tell now, or at all.   (Amis 59)

The verdict would be unfair, since it is based on a few lines taken from a much longer poem. These lines are quoted here only to make a point. Naturally, in practice translators would not base their decision on whether to use rhyme and meter on isolated extracts.

In the following extract from Jonathan Swift's "Daphne," rhyme and meter add considerably to the illocutionary power of the original. Not only does rhyme highlight the technical mastery of the poet; it also adds a tone of levity to the more serious information content:

Ye who hate such inconsistence,
To be easy keep your distance;
Or in folly still befriend her,
But have no concern to mend her.
Lose not time to contradict her,
Nor endeavor to convict her.
                    (Amis 26)

Lewis Carroll's display of virtuosity in "The White Knight's Song" is perhaps more expendable—or is it? A case can be made that the rhyme acts as a genre marker, identifying the poem as belonging to the category of light verse. If rhyme and meter are left untranslated, the genre marker disappears. In cultures familiar with the work of Lewis Carroll, his name alone may act as a genre marker. In cultures not familiar with the author, readers might find it hard to place the poem, unless it is translated into a form immediately recognizable as light verse.

Another reason to mention this poem here is that it is one of the rare examples in English of a rhyme scheme (or, rather, a monorhyme scheme) that approximates the rhyme scheme of the oldest and most venerable canonized genre in Arabic poetry: the qasidah. To be sure, the content of the qasidah has nothing to do with light verse, but the qasidah itself is constructed in strict metrical patterns, with every line ending in the same rhyme sound. This rhyme scheme helps explain why the qasidah is hard to translate and, therefore, why this part of the canonized literature of a great culture remains virtually unknown to the West, even though the West has successfully transposed another Arabic, or, rather, Persian, genre, the ruba'i, by "neutralizing" it as a quatrain.

Again, more about these matters in chapter 3. The lines from Carroll's "White Knight" run as follows:

> Of that old man I used to know—
> Whose look was mild, whose speech was slow,
> Whose hair was whiter than the snow,
> Whose face was very like a crow,
> With eyes, like cinders, all aglow,
> Who seemed distracted with his woe,
> Who rocked his body to and fro,
> And muttered mumblingly and low,
> As if his mouth were full of dough,
> Who snorted like a buffalo—   (Amis 133)

The first three lines of Catullus's second poem read:

> Passer, deliciae meae puellae,
> quicum ludere, quem in sinu tenere,
> cui primum digitum dare appententi.
>
> (Sparrow, darling of my girl
> with whom to play, whom in her bosom to hold,
> to whom desiring to give the tip of her finger.)

Martin translates the lines as follows:

> Sparrow, that art my darling's pet
> My darling's who'll frolic with thee and let
> Thee nestle in her bosom, and when
> Thou peck'st her forefinger will give it again.
>   (4)

Meter has exacted its toll: "that art" in the first line stabilizes Martin's meter, but it loses the directness of Catullus's apposition. The repetition of "My darling" has the same advantage and disadvantage. "Nestle" in line 3 provides a needed foot but adds a connotation not in the original. The elision in "peck'st" is there for metrical reasons. Rhyme has exacted its toll as well: the need to find a word to rhyme with "pet" leads to the enjambment constructed around "let," which also adds a connotation not in the original. The most obvious tribute paid to rhyme is "again" in Martin's fourth line. In Catullus's third line Lesbia simply gives the tip of her finger to the bird; in Martin's fourth line she has to do it "again" because otherwise there would be no rhyme with "when" at the end of line 3.

W. K. Kelly's translation reads as follows:

> Sparrow! my nymph's delicious pleasure!
> Who with thee, her pretty treasure,
> Fanciful in frolic, plays
> Thousand, thousand wanton ways.
>
> (170)

"Nymph" in the first line adds connotations not in the original, but it has probably been selected because it is shorter than "darling," which would result in an unwanted additional foot. The apposition "pretty treasure" stabilizes the meter, but the word "pretty" almost epitomizes everything Catullus wanted not to say in this poem. The third and fourth lines are mere padding, nowhere to be found in the original. They are there to complete a four-line stanza, and they do little else for the poem. "Pleasure" and "treasure" are not the most innovative rhymes, and neither are "plays" and "ways." The repetition of "thousand" in the last line appears to be warranted only by the meter. One is struck by the utter discrepancy between this translation and its original. Yet this translation, too, represented—"was"—Catullus to many readers for many years, unfortunately so because it created an image of Catullus that does not correspond to the original in the least, but understandably so because it represented a Victorian domestication of Catullus, undertaken for mainly ideological reasons.

Sound and Nonsense

If rhyme in a poem can be described as the regulated use of sound effects, the use of other sound effects can be thought of as unregulated. These effects are sometimes onomatopoeic but often also stylized expressions of a certain feeling, mostly joy or sadness. The expressions of joy can often be linked to that stage in the ancestry of poetry when poems were as a matter of course set to music and danced to. The expressions make no sense, by which is meant no exact semantic sense. They do, however, definitely convey a certain emotion. Witness the last line of the following extract taken from the anonymous poem "Hares on the Mountain":

Young women they'll swim like ducks in the water
Young women they'll swim like ducks in the water
If I was a young man I'd go swim all after
To my right fol diddle dero, to my right fol diddle dee.
(Ewart 128)

The nonsense words in the last line seem to indicate that the hypothetical young man swimming after young women is not likely to be upset by the experience. Translators often gratefully use nonsense words to balance the meter in a line. Such words can also serve as a refrain.

Refrains can also be made up of bona fide words that are used out of their ordinary context. The second line of an extract from the anonymous "Scarborough Fair" is an example:

Tell her to plough me an acre of land,
Parsley, sage, rosemary and thyme,
Between the sea and the salt sea strand
And she shall be a true lover of mine.
(Ewart 225)

Translators have to find out whether poetry in the target culture uses nonsense words and expressions. Usually it does, and usually it has ritualized them over time, just as English has done. In that case translators can often just transpose nonsense words and expressions from one tradition into another. They have only to be careful to select words and expressions that fit, or can be made to fit, the meter of the target-language poem. Clearly, any attempt to translate nonsense words and expressions literally is a waste of time.

Nonsense words may be used to add levity of tone to a theme that might otherwise be unacceptable in a culture. In the following extract from Burns's "Green Grow the Rushes"—the bawdy, not the traditional, version—the nonsense "duntie duntie" in combination with the equally nonsensical "O" creates a lilting, festive rhythm that carries the reader to and beyond the potentially more objectionable corresponding non-nonsensical noun, whose effect is weakened in turn by the adjacent second "O":

I dought na speak, yet was na fly'd
My heart play'd duntie duntie, O,

A'ceremonie laid aside,
　I fairly found her cuntie, O.
　　　　　　　　(Ewart 221)

Students can discover the meaning of "duntie duntie" in any collected
Burns, which should also give them the meanings of any other unintelligible words.

It is also possible to construct a poem around the sounds of words as
they rhyme with or echo each other. The semantic meaning is then
made secondary to the sound, thus reversing the "normal" situation.
The resulting poem is automatically characterized as "nonsense poetry."
Again, translators have to investigate the possibilities of constructing
their target language poem around analogous sound sequences. If they
decide to do so, they may have to substitute a different semantic meaning for the one conveyed by some, or even most, words in the original.
The following short poem by Stevie Smith, entitled "The Bereaved
Swan," is a good example:

Wan
Swan
On the lake
Like a cake
Of soap
Why is the swan
Wan
On the lake?
He has abandoned hope.
　　　　　　　　(Grigson 293)

Various translators of Catullus's second poem have tried to render
the sound play of their Latin original, with varying degrees of success.
Louis Zukofsky and Celia Zukofsky translate the "quicum ludere" (with
whom to play) of line 2 as "a thing to delude her." Their translation cap-
tures some of the sound of the original, aided by the fact that a fair part
of English vocabulary is of Romance origin. It also states the very es-
sence of what Catullus believes the bird represents for Lesbia.
　Line 3, "cui primum digitum dare appententi" (to whom desiring to
give the tip of her finger), is translated by Michie as "these / with tantalizing fingertips" (19) and by Tremenheere as "give / a fingertop provoc-
ative" (39). Michie relies on both alliteration (built around the *t* sound)

and assonance constructed around *i*, perhaps highlighted by the contrast with the *ai* in "tantalizing." Tremenheere plays on the assonance of *i* and *o* and to some extent on the alliteration of the *g* in "give" and "fingertop."

"Desiderio mei nitenti" (to my shining desire) in line 5 is translated by Arthur Symons as "my bright / Shining lady of delight" (Aiken 57) and by Horace Gregory as "that radiant lady" (4). The assonance built around the *ai* is obvious in Symons, as is the alliteration built around the *l* sound. Gregory, on the other hand, relies mainly on the *ei* assonance.

Syntax

Syntax is perhaps the most stringent and least flexible of all the constraints translators must work under since it regulates the order of the words to be translated and because few liberties can be taken with that order before the text veers into the unintelligible.

In the following two lines from Graves's poem "Welcome to the Caves of Arta," we hear a Spanish-speaking tour guide explain the wonders of the caves in English, but a kind of English that adheres too closely to Spanish syntax for the reader's comfort:

> You, also, are you capable to make precise in idiom.
>   Considerations magic of illusions wide?
>
> (Amis 232)

This poem has been written with a comical intention. But there have been translators who have seemed to identify the syntax of a language with its "spirit" or some other defining feature and who have accordingly tried to reproduce the syntax of a more prestigious source language in order to "ennoble" the target language.

Syntax affects readers by regulating not just the sequence in which they are given information and exposed to the illocutionary power of the text but also the rhythm at which both information and illocutionary power are dispensed. When in "Young Goodman Brown" Hawthorne writes, "Unfathomable to mere mortals is the love of friends" (Raffel 54), he does so because he wants to emphasize the word "unfathomable" by changing the normal syntactical pattern. Translators can easily reproduce such illocutionary effects by using the same device as long as they translate into another Indo-European language. If they translate into languages without many marked morphological features, such as Chinese, which depend for the successful communication of information on a strict syntactic order, they may find their task much more difficult and they may have to resort to a different device, sanctioned by use in the target language to achieve an analogous effect.

Similarly, the long string of appositions Stevenson uses to describe Utterson, the lawyer in *Dr. Jekyll and Mr. Hyde,* may be hard to reproduce in other languages without loss of informational content or illocutionary effect or both. Utterson is described as "cold, scanty and embarrassed in discourse; backward in sentiment; lean, long, dusty, dreary and yet somehow lovable" (Karl 186–87).

Probably the greatest challenge syntax has in store for translators is that of the construction of the "period," the well-balanced, elegant, sometimes seemingly endless sentence that is so dependent on the syntactical possibilities of the source language that it is almost impossible to reproduce in the target language. The period's information content can always be reproduced simply by splitting it up into a series of sentences of normal length following a normal pattern. But the illocutionary effect of careful, crafted poise always just saved from unintelligibility and incoherence by the next punctuation mark is another matter. Some languages simply give translators no choice at all; others afford them more leeway.

Consider the following period taken from Henry James's short story "The Real Thing":

> When the porter's wife (she used to answer the house-bell) announced: "A gentleman—with a lady, sir," I had, as I often had in those days, for the wish was father to the thought, an immediate vision of sitters.
> (Raffel 222)

One point of this period seems to be to delay information. This aim is achieved by the insertion, first, of the clause between parentheses, then by a succession of clauses, each a little longer than its predecessor. The period also makes a point about character. Since it reproduces the thought process of the protagonist, readers feel they come to know that protagonist not just by being allowed to enter into his thoughts but also by seeing his thinking at work on the page.

The beginning of Catullus's second poem, with its string of appositions, is a syntactic nightmare for translators because such a series, while perfectly acceptable in an inflected language, like Latin, does not sound right in English. The "straightest" rendering of the first two lines, "Passer, deliciae meae puellae / quicum ludere, quem in sinu tenere," is in Kelly's prose translation: "Sparrow, delight of my girl, which she plays with, which she keeps in her bosom" (9–10). It is accurate, mirrors the syntax of the original admirably, and strikes the reader as totally pedestrian. Frederick Raphael and K. McLeish confront the challenge differently, by fundamentally altering the syntax of the original. They translate, "Well, little sparrow, who's my darling's darling then? / Does she like to play with it and hold it in her lap" (25). The result is much more readable in English, but the translators have completely obscured the generic affiliation of the poem: very few readers are likely to suspect that the original was trying to parody a religious hymn. The translators may have thought that considerations of generic affiliation would carry little weight with the vast majority of readers.

Typography

Some writers use typography, the arrangement of words on the page, to achieve illocutionary effect. Typography is always used in poetry, to some extent, but the typography we are interested in here is one that deviates from the typographical tradition in the printing of both prose and poetry.

In prose an obvious typographical device is that of the absence of typographical markers as in Beckett's "Yellow," when the patient asks the nurse where the toilets are in the hospital. The author makes doubly sure readers are alerted to what he is doing by explicitly stating in words what he has already tried to achieve by typography: " 'Oh nurse the W. C. perhaps it might be as well to know.' Like that, all in a rush, without any punctuation" (Karl 458).

In "Peekaboo, I Almost See You," Nash relies on a typographical "gestalt" familiar to everyone who has ever had an eye examination:

> And you look at his chart and it says S H R D Q W E R T Y O P, and you say Well, why S H R D N T L U Q W E R T Y O P? and he says one set of glasses won't do.
> You need two.   (Ewart 450)

In Anthony Brode's "Calypsomania," typography (both colons and capital letters) marks the beat of the calypso:

Now to all criTICS who: quiver like jelly at
The thought of a calypso by: T. S. Eliot,
I wish to STATE that: there are poets and musicians,
Singers also, with: hidden ambitions—
Operatic calypsos: will get society cheers
If COMposed by Britten and sung by Pears.

(Ewart 519)

The passage also exhibits other problems discussed above: off-rhyme in line 2 and an allusion to British music in the last line. If the target audience is familiar with the "calypso," it will get the joke and probably even enjoy it. If not, a footnote could not offer much solace because the item to be explained needs to be heard rather than described. If the audience is familiar with the calypso and uses a Western alphabet into the bargain, translators can easily transpose the typographical elements of the original. If the audience uses a non-Western alphabet, translators have to exploit the typographical conventions connected with that alphabet to achieve analogous effects. They may also have to decide which, if any, target-culture dance could be pronounced analogous to the calypso.

The anonymous "Miss Ellen Gee of Kew" plays on the association between typography and pronunciation. Readers are likely to see a capital letter or series of capital letters printed alone as letters. In this poem, however, the letters, when pronounced, reveal themselves as words or parts of words. The poem might be hard to transpose in anywhere near the same way into languages using different typographical conventions, but the fundamental strategy for writing it should be reproducible, even if the actual devices used turn out to be completely dissimilar. The first stanza of "Miss Ellen Gee at Kew" reads as follows:

Peerless yet hopeless maid of Q,
  Accomplish'd L N G,
Never again shall I and U
  Together sip our T.
For oh! the fates, I know not Y,
  Sent 'midst the flowers a B;
Which ven'mous stung her in the I,
  So that she could not C.

(Grigson 239)

Word and Thing

In *Don Juan,* Byron remarks on the occasion of his fellow poet Southey's predictable, voluminous, and somewhat soporific production:

> I know what our neighbours call longueurs,
>   (We've not so good a word, but have the thing).
>   (Amis 64)

"Longueur" is the term the French use to describe textual passages of respectable length that are unlikely to keep readers' interest or even to keep them awake. Instead of coining an English word, Byron uses the French word because he finds it better suited to the "thing" than any English word. This procedure is technically known as calque or loan translation. Certain things, then, can be expressed most felicitously by words not indigenous to a writer's language. Alternatively, certain things and the words used for them can be very closely identified with a given culture—so much so, in fact, that they are difficult to transpose into another.

In the poem "Every Day Characters: Portrait of a Lady" W. M. Praed addresses a lady as follows:

> Where were you finished? tell me where!
>   Was it at Chelsea, or at Chiswick?   (Amis 94)

He uses the word "finished" to refer to the typically British institution of the "finishing school," where young ladies used to acquire the polish that would enable them to function well in society.

Some of these culture-bound words and concepts can be transposed by analogy; others simply have to be "calqued," that is, taken over into the target text and perhaps explained in a note. Translators have to base their strategy on the degree to which the target cultures are familiar with the concepts denoted. Sherwood Anderson may face translators with an insoluble problem in the following passage taken from his short story "Queer": "[H]is eyes were blue with the colorless blueness of the marbles called aggies that the boys of Winesburg carried in their pockets" (Raffel 450).

Rose Terry Cooke tries to define the word she uses as the title of her short story "Grit" but to no obvious avail for translators: "But his share of 'grit' was not simply endurance, perseverance, dogged persistence, and courage, but a most unlimited obstinacy and full faith in his own wisdom" (Raffel 164). Translators will still find it difficult to translate "grit"; they may just have to "calque" it.

The Spartan herald in Aristophanes's *Lysistrata* carries what is called a "Skutala Lakōnika" in the original. The anonymous translator (or translators) of *The Eleven Comedies* transliterates the word as "a Lacedaemonian 'skytale' " (279) and describes the thing in the following lengthy footnote: "A staff in use among the Lacedaemonians for writing cipher dispatches. A strap of leather or paper was wound round the 'skytale,' on which the required message was written lengthwise, so that when unrolled it became unintelligible; the recipient abroad had a staff of the same thickness and pattern, and so was enabled by rewinding the document to decipher the words" (279).

In what follows I list the efforts made by various translators to "acculturate" the thing in question, to perform the almost impossible task of finding a word for a thing that their audience has no concept of. "A Spahtan scroll-stick" (Sutherland 37) and "a standard Spartan cipher-rod" (Sommerstein 221) do not conjure up an image of the thing, nor is it likely that they will mean much to the reader or spectator without any knowledge of the way secret messages were transmitted in Greek antiquity. "A Spartan secret dispatch" (Dickinson 114) is much clearer, as is Fitts's "A scroll / with a message from Spahta" (90), but neither conveys anything of the way in which the message was carried. Lindsay opts for the first solution with "my dispatch cane" (94), while Parker goes back to the solution chosen by the translator(s) of *The Eleven Comedies*. He translates "a Spartan epistle" (70), and adds a footnote. Only Way's "a Spartan baton" (44) can be said to have missed the point altogether: the thing he has in mind is nothing like the thing Aristophanes mentions, and the word is certain to call forth all kinds of associations in the reader's or spectator's mind, none presumably coming very close to the thing referred to in the original text.

Works Cited

Aiken, W. A., ed. *The Poems of Catullus.* New York: Dutton, 1950.

Amis, Kingsley, ed. *The New Oxford Book of Light Verse.* Oxford: Oxford UP, 1987.

Anonymous, trans. *Aristophanes: The Eleven Comedies.* London: Athenian Soc., 1912.

Dickinson, Patrick, trans. *Aristophanes.* London: Oxford UP, 1970.

Ewart, Gavin, ed. *The Penguin Book of Light Verse.* Harmondsworth, Eng.: Penguin, 1986.

Fitts, Dudley, trans. *Lysistrata*. New York: Harcourt, 1954.

Goold, George P., trans. *Catullus*. London: Duckworth, 1983.

Gregory, Horace, trans. *The Poems of Catullus*. New York: Norton, 1956.

Grigson, Geoffrey, ed. *The Faber Book of Nonsense Verse*. London: Faber, 1987.

Harrison, T. W., and J. Simmons, trans. Aikin Mata: *The Lysistrata of Aristophanes*. Ibadan: Oxford UP, 1966.

Hickie, W. J., trans. *The Comedies of Aristophanes*. London: Bell, 1902.

Housman, Lawrence, trans. *Lysistrata*. London: Women's, 1911.

Hull, William, trans. *The Catullus of William Hull*. Calcutta: Lake Gardens, 1968.

Karl, Frederick R., ed. *The Signet Classic Book of British Short Stories*. New York: NAL, 1985.

Kelly, W. K., trans. *The Poems of Catullus and Tibullus*. London: Bell, 1906.

Lindsay, Jack, trans. *Lysistrata*. Garden City: Halcyon, 1950.

Martin, Theodore, trans. *The Poems of Catullus*. Edinburgh: Blackwood, 1875.

Michie, James, trans. *The Poems of Catullus*. New York: Random, 1969.

Mills, Barriss, trans. *The Carmina of Catullus*. West Lafayette: Purdue UP, 1965.

Parker, Douglass, trans. *Lysistrata*. Ann Arbor: U of Michigan P, 1964.

Raffel, Burton, ed. *The Signet Classic Book of American Short Stories*. New York: NAL, 1985.

Raphael, Frederick, and K. McLeish, trans. *The Poems of Catullus*. London: Cape, 1978.

Rogers, Benjamin, trans. *The Comedies of Aristophanes*. London: Bell, 1911.

Sesar, Carl, trans. *Selected Poems of Catullus*. New York: Mason, 1974. N. pag.

Sommerstein, Alan, ed. *Aristophanes:* The Acharnians. The Clouds. Lysistrata. Harmondsworth, Eng.: Penguin, 1972.

Sutherland, Donald, trans. *Lysistrata*. San Francisco: Chandler, 1961.

Tremenheere, J. H. A., trans. *The Lesbia of Catullus*. London: Fisher, 1897.

Way, Arthur S., trans. *Aristophanes*. London: Macmillan, 1934.

Wheelwright, Arthur, trans. *The Comedies of Aristophanes*. Oxford: Talboys, 1837.

Whigham, Peter, trans. *The Poems of Catullus*. Harmondsworth, Eng.: Penguin, 1966.

Zukofsky, Louis, and Celia Zukofsky, trans. *Catullus*. London: Cape Goliard, 1969. N. pag.

Chapter 3
Text

From Passage to Text

In chapter 2 we studied isolated passages from many texts, selected because they illustrated the most common problems of illocutionary language use that translators face. Yet writers do not write just passages of texts; they compose whole texts, and translators therefore need to translate whole texts. In doing so, they can put to good use the skills acquired while learning to translate isolated passages.

Texts are not written in a vacuum. Like language, literature preexists its practitioners. Writers are born into a certain culture at a certain time. They inherit that culture's language, its literary traditions (its poetics), its material and conceptual characteristics (microwaves and the ideas of Sigmund Freud in twentieth-century American culture; chamber pots and the ideas of the Enlightenment in eighteenth-century England)—in a word, its "universe of discourse"—and its standards.

This is not to say that writers are the captives of the culture they write in; on the contrary, they can write within the parameters set by that culture or they can try to bend them or even go beyond them. Neither the poetics nor the ideology of a culture is monolithic. Rather they consist of one dominant current and various countercurrents or peripheral currents. Both the poetics and the ideology of a culture are marked by tension and struggle between the center and the periphery, with various outcomes. Sometimes the center reasserts its domination; sometimes the periphery takes over or at least dislodges the center. Christianity was the prevailing ideology of the European Middle Ages, but it always had to battle various heresies. It was able to reassert its domination until the Reformation, when its center was split. Later on, it would become one of many potential centers.

Similarly, medieval non-Latin poetry owed little to the poetry of antiquity but much to the poetry of Provence. Poetry produced on the Provençal model in the various languages of Europe was considered "good" and "refined"—dominant—as opposed to the more "uncouth" popular poetry of the times. The Renaissance dislodged poetry written on the Provençal model from the center and replaced it with poetry based on models from classical antiquity.

The Four Levels of Translation

Until now we have only considered problems arising on one of the four levels listed above: the level of language or, rather, the level of illocutionary language use. Yet problems also arise on the levels of universe of discourse, poetics, and ideology. Translators have to develop strategies to deal with those problems. It may be possible to establish a hierarchy of levels, of problems translators consider more weighty than other problems or of problems they need to solve before they can go on to solve other problems. That hierarchy might look like this, in descending order of importance: (1) ideology, (2) poetics, (3) universe of discourse, (4) language. This hierarchy runs counter to the commonly established prejudices regarding translation, which is often considered a mere matter of substituting one word or phrase for another, but it can be shown to make sense.

Translators are interested in getting their work published. This will be accomplished much more easily if it is not in conflict with standards for acceptable behavior in the target culture: with that culture's ideology. If the source text clashes with the ideology of the target culture, translators may have to adapt the text so that the offending passages are either severely modified or left out altogether.

Translations will also be published, sold, and read more easily if they correspond or can be made to correspond to the dominant concept of literature in the target culture. For that reason the unrhymed poetry of Western antiquity was, as we have seen, routinely translated into rhyming poetry in Europe and the Americas from the sixteenth to the nineteenth century.

Finally, certain features of the author's universe of discourse may have become unintelligible to the target audience, either because they no longer exist or because they have acquired different meanings. Translators must either substitute analogous features from the target culture's universe of discourse or try to re-create the author's universe of discourse as best they can in a preface, in footnotes, or—what is most frequently done—in both.

Ideology, Poetics, Universe of Discourse

Writers, then, never directly describe an experience or express an emotion, no matter what Romantic poetics and its successors may assert to the contrary. What writers describe or express is always filtered through a poetics and a universe of discourse. Translators face problems on both counts. It is eminently possible that the experience expressed or the situation described, while ideologically acceptable in the source culture, is not, or is no longer, felt to be acceptable in the target culture. Over the last century and a half, for instance, many translators simply omitted from their translations the poem we shall be using as the focal point for our discussion. They felt that the situation described would be ideologically unacceptable to members of their culture, who would most likely consider it obscene.

This is as good a point as any to invoke the indulgence of readers who might have the same reaction to the poem in question. Suffice it to say that I have chosen to discuss this original and its many translations not to titillate students but to highlight the many strategies translators use to deal with an "ideologically doubtful" original.

Once translators have decided either to leave the original untranslated for ideological reasons or to use a specific strategy to translate it after all, they face problems concerning poetics and universe of discourse. Sometimes a genre cannot easily be transplanted into another literature or another culture. In the source literature the genre may automatically trigger a set of expectations in its readers that will not be present in the readers of the translation. Alternatively, readers of the translation may approach that translation with a totally unsuitable set of expectations based on their experience of reading analogous works in their own literature. More is said about this situation in chapter 4.

On the universe-of-discourse level, translators may be faced with things, customs, and concepts that were immediately intelligible to the readers of the original but are no longer intelligible to prospective readers of the translation. Fortunately, there appears to be some level of human experience, emotion, and material and philosophical civilization on which translators can respond to the original and which they can use as a point of departure in their search for analogs in their own culture and literature. The situation described in the poem to be discussed here is such a "human universal," which is subject to different rituals and conventions in different cultures. Similarly, the clothes of the person speaking in the poem have analogs in most cultures, as do the parts of the house he refers to.

Translators have to make decisions over and over again on the levels of ideology, poetics, and universe of discourse, and those decisions are always open to criticism from readers who subscribe to a different ideology; who are convinced of the superiority of the poetics dominant in their time and culture; and who are dissatisfied with the strategies translators have chosen to make universe-of-discourse elements intelligible or more easy to intuit.

On this matter there is no court of appeal. Ultimately a consensus arises on the value of a given translation, but that consensus, too, can change. Famous translations of the past have faded into oblivion, and new translations that were found objectionable when first published have taken their place, or at least taken a place alongside them. The history of Bible translation in Europe affords many examples of this process.

Text: Catullus 32

Let us now look at the specific text I have chosen to illustrate the foregoing points: Catullus's thirty-second poem. I give the Latin original with an interlinear translation. Under every word or phrase in the Latin is its semantic English equivalent. Interlinear translations operate strictly on the semantic level of language use and make no attempt at illocutionary language use. I next isolate the problems that occur on the four levels listed above and show how different translators have tried to solve them.

The text reads as follows:

1 Amabo,   mea   dulcis   Ipsitilla
  Please,   my   sweet   Ipsitilla

2 Meae deliciae,   mei   lepores,
  My   delights,   my   charms,

3 Iube   ad te veniam   meridiatum
  Command to you I should come at noon

4 Et si iusseris,   illud adiuvato
  And if you command, it would be of help

5 Nequis liminis   obseret   tabellam
  Nobody of the threshold if would close the door panel

6 Neu tibi lubeat   foras abire
  Nor to you it might be pleasing outside to walk off

7 Sed domi maneas,   paresque   nobis
  But at home you would stay, you would prepare also for us

8 Novem continuas fututiones
  Nine continuous fuckifications

9 Verum, si quid   agis,   statim iubeto
  Well then, if anything you will do, at once order me

10 Nam pransus iaceo et   satur   supinus
   For   stuffed I lie and satiated on my back

11 Pertundo   tunicamque palliumque.
   I thrust through "tunic" and   "pallium" too.

The poem is addressed to a woman called Ipsitilla. The name itself is some kind of a pun or even joke. *Ipse*, literally meaning "herself," is also the word slaves used for their mistresses. *Illa* is the female form of the third person of the deictic pronoun and can be translated as "that one." No one who has tried to translate Catullus 32 over the last century and a half has even tried to find an analog for the name, probably because they were daunted by the combination of linguistic categories and universe-of-discourse elements that comes close to the untranslatable. "My very own mistress" sounds rather tame, in part because it has been used so much in the target literature since roughly 1600. Maybe something like "Mistrissima" comes a little closer.

In the poem the speaker has eaten breakfast, maybe even in bed, since the word "pallium" refers to a kind of poncho the Romans both wore as clothing and used as a blanket. He is planning his day, and a visit—of an obvious kind—to Ipsitilla is high on the agenda. The poem is a parody of a billet-doux, usually sent to arrange a meeting of lovers. But love does not enter into the matter here, since Ipsitilla is obviously a certain kind of professional, a Roman prostitute. The speaker wants a tryst with Ipsitilla, and he wants an answer fast because he has an erection so huge that his penis bursts through his clothes (and, possibly, blankets).

Text and Ideology

Let us now supplement the interlinear translation with the translation in the Loeb Classical Library series. It has been used by generations of students and scholars as a "faithful" translation that tries to make available the semantic information content of the original and does not try to function as a literary text. It is obvious from the "faithful" translation quoted here that the concept of faithful is in need of some revision:

> I entreat you, my sweet Ipsitilla, my darling, my charmer, bid me come and rest at noonday with you. And if you bid me, grant me this kindness too, that no one may bar the panel of your threshold, nor you yourself have a fancy to go away, but stay at home. . . . But if you will at all, then bid me come at once. . . .   (38)

First published in 1913, and revised in 1950, the translation has been repeatedly reprinted. Because the translator has not translated the whole poem, he has clearly not been faithful to the source text, certainly not on the level of language. The translator himself probably felt justified in exercising "selective" faithfulness on that level because of overriding ideological reasons, thinking that the passages in question would not be considered acceptable in his culture at the time he produced the translation. In other words, the decisions the translator made on the level of language were based on criteria found not on that level but on the hierarchically higher level of ideology.

Text and Poetics

There is no problem on the level of poetics because, as said above, the series in which the translation appears, the Loeb Classical Library, is known to provide scholars and students not with "literary translations," that is, translations that try to take their place as literature, but with "translations of literature," that is, "literal" ("faithful") translations designed merely to facilitate the understanding of the source text.

A few more remarks about the text: At the time Catullus wrote, younger poets were subscribing to a new poetics, one that took its bearings more from the mostly lyrical, short and epigrammatic, elegant, witty, and "daringly" erotic Greek poetry produced in Alexandria than from the mostly epic, often interminably long, plodding, serious, moralistic, and patriotic poetry produced by their immediate Roman predecessors. Catullus led the way in embracing this "imported" poetics, and his poetry has helped it move from the periphery of Latin literature to the center.

As we have seen, the poem is a billet-doux of a very particular kind. Ipsitilla seems to be not the blushing beloved to whom billets-doux are traditionally addressed but, instead, a professional in the realms of love: witness the warning against schedule conflicts in lines 5 and 6, the rather direct tone and the specific content of the request made in line 8, and the somewhat obscene description of the ardent lover in lines 10 and 11.

Although Catullus may well have written actual billets-doux to various women in the Rome of his time—even to Lesbia—he incorporated the form into his poetry only this once, suggesting a deliberate act on his part. The poem represents a blow struck in the struggle between the old poetics and the new. The old poetics would not have found the subject of Catullus's thirty-second poem fit for poetry. And that may explain why Catullus wrote a mock billet-doux and included it in his book of poems: to shock readers who subscribed to the old poetics and make them aware of the new. By turning the run-of-the-mill billet-doux into an Alexandrian-style epigram, Catullus demonstrated the flexibility of the new poetics as compared with the old, not to mention the "flexibility" of the new morality (ideology) as compared with the old. On the levels of both poetics and ideology Catullus was writing outside the parameters set by the dominant ideology and the dominant poetics. He was challenging them—and not too subtly, either—by electing to write about an experience not generally accepted as worthy of literature and by filtering that experience through a new genre, considered frivolous and obscene by many potential readers.

The Cultural Status of the Text and the Passage of Time

Translators need to understand the position of the source text in the source literature and the source culture; without such knowledge they cannot cast around for the relevant analogies in the target literature and the target culture. For this reason, among others, scholars should translate, and translations should be considered works of creativity *and* scholarship: scholars are much more likely to be familiar with the literary-historical and cultural context of the source text than nonscholars are. I do not say that all scholars can translate or that all translators should be scholars; I do say, though, that scholars who can translate should do so and should be recognized for their work by the community of scholars at large.

Yet even if translators are knowledgeable enough to look for relevant analogies in the target culture, they may not be able to find them. Much depends on the cultural status of the source text. If, like Catullus, the author of the source text is regarded as a classic, his or her works may be approached with a mixture of awe and reverence that could act to obscure their subversive origins. Those elements of Catullus 32 that do not fit the image of the classic but were instrumental in making him famous are likely to be left out, both in individual poems (as in the "faithful" translation quoted above) and in his oeuvre as a whole: many translations passing themselves off as the complete Catullus omit poem 32 and a few others.

The comparative success of a genre is also a complicating factor: the Alexandrian epigram that was relatively new to Rome and to Roman readers when Catullus (and the other "new" poets he befriended) used it for the first time has since gone on to a long and distinguished career, not just in Latin (and Hellenistic Greek) literature but in all the literatures of Europe. Translators therefore can not hope to recapture its pristine newness, unless they abandon it as a genre altogether and replace it by a "new" genre that may have an analogous effect on the readers of the target text. The following translation is a good illustration of this strategy:

Intention: Love

My dear sweet Ipsitilla,
My pet, you're the very girl:
Have me report to you this pip emma.
If the answer's Roger, be sure
(a) No one bolts your door before I do
(b) You don't get an itch to go roaming.
I want you indoors,
With nine complete plans of campaign.
The exercise? Fucking by numbers.
So: if you're on, send a runner.
I've had my meal and I'm in the picture:
Lying here stiff at attention
Bashing holes in my Number One Dress.
   (Raphael and McLeish 47–48)

Like Catullus, the translators have tried to incorporate into the literature of their time a text type not usually thought of as literary. What Catullus did to the billet-doux they do to the military directive, here the military directive written in the style of the British army and culminating in the phrase "nine complete plans of campaign." Consequently they also use British army jargon, such as "pip emma," "Roger," "send a runner," "at attention," and "Number One Dress." Students should try to find out the meaning of these instances of "professiolect." Like Catullus's original, the translation acquires its illocutionary effect by playing on at least two registers—juxtaposed most obviously in the "stiff at attention" of the penultimate line—and by radically mismatching utterance and situation. The translators routinely eschew literal semantic renditions of words and phrases in the original, trying instead to achieve matching illocutionary power with different words and phrases belonging to the target culture.

Since the translation was published in 1978, the translators obviously felt there was no need to adapt the original to the ideological presuppositions of the target culture: what was not too obscene for the Romans of Catullus's time was thought not too obscene for the English-speaking readers of the 1970s. The Loeb Classical Library translator made a different decision fifty years earlier—rightly if he just wanted his translation published, wrongly if he really wanted it to be a faithful translation.

Translation Strategies

No other translators of Catullus's thirty-second poem have gone as far as Raphael and McLeish in the last century and a half. They have all produced short poems evidently designed to fit in with the poetics dominant at the time the translation was published. Nine translations rhyme, nine have been written in free verse and two in prose. Most of the translations published before 1950 rhyme. The first translation in free verse was published in 1956; the "last" translation in rhyme in 1959. Between 1956 and 1969 free verse reigns, but rhyme reenters the stage from 1970 onward. Translations published during the last two decades alternate between rhyme and free verse. Translators who use rhyme after 1969 may be doing so because rhyme paired with modern, as opposed to Victorian or Georgian, diction allows them to have their cake and eat it: the rhyme can serve to mark the "classical," or at any rate "older," status of the text, and the diction makes it acceptable to the poetics dominant after 1970, which admits of both rhyme and free verse.

Before we analyze the original and the translations on the level of illocutionary use of language, it is important to reiterate what has been demonstrated above: translators do not just translate words; they also translate a universe of discourse, a poetics, and an ideology. Moreover, their decision whether or not to translate something is likely to be based much more on considerations of the levels of ideology (ethically or politically dangerous or unacceptable) and poetics, (no equivalent available in the target culture; attempts to introduce an analog may prejudice the eventual publication of the translation) than on the level of illocutionary use of language or universe of discourse. In other words, translators tend to reach decisions on the translatability of a given work on a level that is much more encompassing, more "global," than that of illocutionary language use. Translatable does not always mean worth translating. Texts that are worth translating and have achieved a certain renown in their culture of origin are not necessarily all translated, for a variety of reasons, usually both ideological and poetological.

Once translators decide they are going to translate a text, they try to fit it into the target culture. Perhaps the text offers something felt to be lacking in the target culture. Usually that lack is not felt in absolute terms. Texts so radically different from target culture texts that no remote analogy can be suggested for them stand a slim chance of being translated for any but a scholarly audience. Catullus 32 easily fits in with English and American culture of the seventies and eighties: short poems are still written as a matter of course. Patriotic epics of the kind written by Catullus's immediate predecessors are a different matter. The best that can be hoped for them is a translation in prose for a fairly restricted specialist audience—a "translation of literature." There is no point in even trying to produce a "literary" translation of these epics, because the poetics of the target culture no longer recognizes them as literature.

Yet there are other writers of the Greek and Roman epic whose work is recognized as literature in the target culture: Vergil, for instance, or Homer. This body of work raises another problem for translators: certain writers are labeled as great authors of world literature and have been incorporated into a canon not subject to the vagaries of time or the geographical accident of birth. To be considered culturally literate, members of the target culture must have at least some knowledge of the works of those great writers and the works are, accordingly, taught in the culture's educational institutions. This fact creates what amounts to a permanent audience for those works, which are, as a result, regularly retranslated. Catullus's immediate predecessors, the epic poets Naevius and Ennius, never acquired the status of great authors, and translators trying to decide whether to translate them have to weigh the absence of a permanent audience.

The Weight of Traditional Interpretations of Writers and Their Texts

Besides being universally recognized as great, writers may be known as exemplary practitioners of a certain aspect of the craft of writing. Catullus, for instance, has always been famous for his mellifluous line, his sound effects. This type of label is important because it can mean that readers prejudge the image of the writer. Catullus is memorable for more than his sound or his love lyrics, but these are what he is best known for. Such public images reduce the complexity of the person they label, but like most labels they also stick. Translators have to decide whether to make their translation conform to the author's preexisting image or to translate him or her in such a way that they expose the image as reductionist and reveal a new X or Y.

In translating Catullus, the Zukofskys have taken the first strategy to extremes. Because Catullus excels at sound effects, their argument runs, the translation should expose the English reader first and foremost to the sound of Catullus while treating his meaning more as an afterthought. Accordingly, the Zukofskys have looked for English words that, pronounced the American way, re-create the string of sounds produced by the Latin. The first two lines of the Zukofskys' translation of poem 32 illustrate their strategy:

> I'm a bow, my dual kiss, Ipsithilla,
> my daily key, my eye's little leap-horse.

At first, the meaning is not obvious, and "Ipsithilla" is the only sound string that is recognizable. But if readers read the lines aloud with one eye on the Latin text, they soon notice that "I'm a bow" corresponds to "Amabo," "my dual kiss" to "mea dulcis," "my daily key" to "meae deliciae" and "my eye's little leap-horse" to "mei lepores." Even meaning is not altogether absent if readers do not limit themselves to the most obvious meanings of the words. The speaker of the poem could be stretched by ardent love into a "bow," meaning the weapon used by Roman archers, but "bow" can also mean "yoke" and might be used here as metonymy for the state the lover is in. Both meanings would suit the ironic tone of the original, the "yoke" perhaps better than the "bow." Similarly, the noun "leap" can also mean "an act of covering a female animal," which would fit in well with the casual obscenities dropped elsewhere in Catullus 32. The image of the speaker being stretched as a bow fits in with another label stuck on Catullus, that of the lover suffering from the betrayal of his mistress and eventually destroyed by it. Catullus's famous "Odi et amo" epigram has given many commentators the license to interpret the rest of his love poetry accordingly. The "stretching" suggested by the Zukofskys' "bow" is obviously different, but readers familiar with the "odi et amo" label will accept this interpretation more easily.

Translators have to gauge the extent to which individual works of a frequently translated author are read and interpreted in the light of his or her whole oeuvre, a situation not unlike the one they face when during the translation process they check separate chunks of text against the whole of the text. Does the totality of an oeuvre label the author in a certain way? Is that label generally accepted? Is it wise to challenge it or is it wiser to translate accordingly, even if acceptance of the label (Catullus the long-suffering lover, for instance) detracts from possible readings of other parts of the writer's oeuvre in a different light (Catullus the political poet, for instance, or Catullus the chronicler of his time)? If translators accept the overall label, they can then smuggle allusions to it into translations of parts of the oeuvre that are not necessarily covered by it, as the Zukofskys have done in their translation of Catullus 32.

Translation Tactics: The Illocutionary Level

Once translators have decided where to position the source text in the target culture and the target literature, they have to solve the problems dealt with in chapter 1 of this book. We therefore now proceed to identify them and to comment on various solutions, but it should be obvious that translators do not start solving those problems first, except in a teaching situation. When they are translating in the real world, they solve these problems on the basis of the solutions they have devised for the hierarchically more important problems that arise on the levels of ideology and poetics. Or, to put it differently, one last time: translators first develop a strategy for translating a whole text; on the basis of that strategy they develop tactical solutions for problems in various chunks of that text.

The problems that arise on the level of illocutionary use of language in Catullus 32 can be subsumed under the categories outlined in chapter 2. In addition, some translators have made use of categories described there to "compensate" for their inability to provide an analog in every instance. Finally, some problems arise on the level of universe of discourse.

Cultural Allusion

"Pertundo" in the last line of the original carries a cultural allusion. The verb itself means something like "to pierce through," but the Romans also worshipped a "Dea Pertunda," a goddess called Pertunda, whose task it was to oversee the successful perforation of hymens. None of the translators surveyed here have tried to render the cultural allusion, which adds a certain touch of piquancy to the obscenity: Ipsitilla, being a professional in matters of love, has little current use for the ministrations of the goddess Pertunda. Today translators into English might take the name of Dr. Ruth here, and not in vain. Of course they would still have to combine the cultural allusion with a verbal shape (its grammatical category is not important) that either exists or can be made to exist in English.

Translators have hit on different solutions for the problem raised by "pertundo," and their solutions are based on ideological considerations. The somewhat obscene description of an erection was not considered acceptable as such before the "liberated" sixties. Earlier translators have recourse to euphemisms, some veering off into poetic diction, others not. A 1948 translation reads, "my tunic monstrously awry" (Lindsay), whereas a 1959 translation has, "watching my tunic stand up straight" (Swanson 31), both rather unremarkable euphemisms. Other translations, published in 1956 and 1957, use euphemisms belonging to the level of poetic diction: "my tree of life (your bedfellow) / has risen joyfully tearing through my clothes" (Gregory 42) and "and feel / love knocking, beating at my passion's door" (Copley 31). Translations published in the sixties and later rise to the requisite level of obscenity or even, arguably, beyond it. A 1966 translation has, "with jutting cock" (Whigham 89); a 1967 translation has, "the thing sticks out of my tunic" (Sisson 49); and a 1970 translation reads, "Feeling my pecker stand up straight" (Myers and Ormsby 38), maybe the only attempt that achieves a fraction of the irony conveyed in the original's allusion to Pertunda.

Literary Allusion: Word and Thing

"Tunicamque palliumque" in the last line of the original carries both a literary allusion and universe-of-discourse connotations. The suffix "-que" repeated at the end of the last two words in a line is a hallmark of the style of Naevius and Ennius, whose epic poetics Catullus rebelled against. Using a stylistic feature marked by the moralistic and patriotic epic in a poem like 32 amounts to parody pure and simple. None of the translators surveyed have tried to reproduce the parodistic intentions of the original at all.

On the universe-of-discourse or word-thing level "tunica" and "pallium" present a problem. Most translators render them as "tunic" and "cloak" or "gown," as in Burton's spirited (though suffering from the tyranny of rhyme) version:

> For dinner-full I lie aback
> And gown and tunic through I crack.

"Tunica" is not really a "tunic" in the modern English sense of the word, and "pallium" is certainly not a "cloak" or "gown." Latin-English dictionaries give the impression that a *tunica* is a standard unisex undergarment, different for men and women only in length, whereas a *pallium* can be both a garment somewhat like the Mexican poncho and a bed cover. Dorothea Wender, being a Latin scholar, simply gives a calque of the original:

> And think I should mention
> My tunic and my pallium
> Are standing at attention.
>   (10)

The following tactical solutions show the influence of strategies ruling the production of the translation as a whole. A 1974 translation has, "blasting through my underwear for you" (Sesar), probably a somewhat belated tribute to the liberated sixties, but in any case a perfect example of the application, on the illocutionary level, of a decision arrived at on the ideological level. A similar example is provided by Raphael and McLeish's "Bashing holes in my Number One Dress." We know which global strategy is responsible for this tactical decision. We also know the strategy behind the Zukofskys' translation of the last two lines of poem 32 as:

> [H]e's primed now a joke-stuffed satyr so pin us!
> pert under the tunic, pulling up the quilt.

The translation "satyr so pin us" is a felicitous rendering of "satur supinus" and "pert under the tunic" is an equally felicitous rendering of "pertundo tunicamque." The other two half lines appear to be wider off the mark.

Grammar

Translators sometimes change the grammatical categories of the original text to express the same basic information, though with a different illocutionary effect. Perhaps the most striking example is Whigham's translation of the verb "pertundo" in the last line of Catullus 32 by the nominal phrase "with jutting cock." W. A. Aiken completely changes the grammatical categories in line 5 but still conveys the same information.

His "then bar your friendly gates to all beside" (43) can be said to "correspond" to the original's "Nequis liminis obseret tabellam" (if nobody would bar the door panel of your threshold). In both Aiken's translation and the original the information is that the speaker wants to be inside with Ipsitilla and that he wants all other potential visitors outside for the duration of his visit. One may ask why Aiken feels he has to go to such lengths to convey the same information. The answer, a common one, is contained in one word: rhyme. Aiken's next line reads, "myself; don't let a foolish whim to ride." The irony is that the rhyme word "ride" is nowhere to be found in the original.

Scenes and Frames

We now come to another intriguing aspect of the translation process; the correlation, or lack thereof, between "scenes" and "frames." First introduced into the study of semantics (Fillmore), the concepts have recently been made productive for the study of the translation process (Vannerem and Snell-Hornby). The basic idea is that the frame is the linguistic form of the utterance, whereas the scene is the personal experience that gives rise to the frame. The writer starts from a scene and produces a frame. Translators face the frame on the page, and they may try to reconstruct the scene that activated it. Interesting possibilities arise when translators do not activate the same scene that activated the author's frame because of temporal or spatial cultural differences.

Aiken translates line 6 as "don't let a foolish whim to ride / abroad remove you from my sight, but stay" (43). The original merely says something like "nor may it please you to go off outside." Aiken's scene may fit the New England of the forties, where ladies would go for a ride in the afternoon, on horseback or in cars; it definitely does not fit Rome in the final decades of the Republic, where ladies simply did not ride in the city, if at all. They would be carried around in litters.

F. A. Wright translates the same line as "Be sure you don't a shopping go" (124)—the unnecessary inversion being once again caused by the pressure of rhyme. His scene appears to be the one men of a certain generation or a certain frame of mind almost automatically associate with the main reason for women to leave their houses. Lindsay gives us a similar translation: "and don't rush out to call or shop." He adds the other traditional reason for women to leave their houses: to visit other women and waste time in endless conversation. F. O. Copley betrays yet another scene in his rendering of the line: "no note 'gone out back soon' " (31). Needless to say, the frame we find in the original provides no justification for any of these scenes. We simply do not know which scene in Catullus's experience may have triggered the frame in line 6 of poem 32. In view of what we know of the poem, it is possible that there is no experience, no scene behind it at all, that the frame is simply the result of a literary finger exercise. Yet this does not stop translators from inventing all kinds of scenes and passing them off as being in the original.

Evasive Tactics

Translators' adaptation of the original on ideological grounds gives rise to evasive devices ranging from poetic circumlocution to the more prosaic footnote. In the first device translators exploit poetic diction to substitute vague terms for the all too precise terms in the original that spell ideological trouble. In the second device they exploit the explanatory function of the footnote to supply some anodyne "explanation" that greatly weakens the objectionable words in the original. Aiken translates the last two lines of Catullus 32 as:

> [B]y you I'd eager stand, as here I lie
> alone, full-surfeited, aroused aflame to fire
> the furnace of reciprocal desire.   (43)

Aiken also exploits all the other features poetic diction has to offer the obfuscating translator: alliteration (constructed around the *f* sound), rhyme and assonance constructed around initial *a* sounds. Whether the "stand" in his first line is designed to match the irony of "pertundo" will probably remain moot.

George Lamb and James Grainger, whose translation of Catullus "in metrical verse" was published in one volume with W. Kelly's prose translation, sidestep all possible ideological complications by rendering Catullus's last two lines with the vague and innocuous

> Speed thee, wanton, fair and free!
> Tell me I must haste to thee.
>   (200)

They too exploit the possibilities of alliteration (constructed around the *f* sound), assonance (constructed around the *ee*), and rhyme. The "thee" form, already somewhat archaic to Victorian ears, is probably there not only to rhyme with "free" but also to emphasize the "timelessness" of the

original. Following Robert Browning and others, many Victorian translators believed that the timelessness of the classics could best be ren-
dered by means of slightly archaic diction.

Kelly translates line 3 as follows (in prose): "bid me like a dear girl to
pass the noon"; he goes on to supply the following footnote to explain
"noon": "that is, to take my siesta with you" (30). Needless to say, a "siesta" is hardly the activity the speaker is interested in. It cannot be repeated enough, however, that these tactical decisions on the level of
language have not been prompted by the translators' sudden lack of
knowledge of Latin. Rather, they are based on strategic decisions made
on a hierarchically higher level.

Neologism

Catullus 32 contains one famous neologism: the plural noun "fututiones" in line 8. The neologism is constructed on the basis of the verb
futuo, which expresses lovemaking, but in a register much closer to that
represented by an English verb beginning with the same *f* sound. Catullus drops the *o* at the end of the verb and adds the suffix *-tio*, which
is usually found only in connection with lofty abstract concepts such as
imagina-tio or *adora-tio*. Catullus then adds the *nes*, which the grammatical constraints of Latin force him to do since *nes* is the normal marker
for the plural of nouns of this category.

The word *fututio*, the singular of *fututiones*, represents a clash of registers in and by itself: one component is the low-sociolect *futu(o)*, the
other the high-professiolect *-tio*. It is almost impossible to come up with
an English analog for this concoction. Two of the least implausible ones
might be "fuckification" and "screwery."

If we keep the ideological level of strategic decision making in mind,
it comes as no surprise that many of the older translators do not even try
to render this word. Instead, they deploy the familiar strategies of ob-
fuscation. First the footnote: Kelly's translation, "no end of amorous delights," is supplemented by the somewhat cryptic statement, "We have
substituted a vague phrase for a singularly plain and precise one" (30).
Then the vagueness sanctioned by poetic diction: Lamb and Grainger
offer, "But prepare thy charms to aid / Every frolic love e'er play'd."

Aiken uses the same basic idiom but introduces a slightly more
"daring" verb: "[T]ill each intemperate frolic love can play / has been
engorged by us nine times" (43).

Copley uses another familiar and faintly suggestive euphemism:
"nine times to feel the pulse of love" (31), and Gregory's "nine long

bouts of love" (42) begins to leave poetic diction as such behind without lapsing into Lindsay's totally anodyne "nine hugs without a stop." Michie tries to infuse some of the Catullan irony into his translation of the line by constructing it around the metaphor of the play and punning in the meantime on at least two of the meanings of both "play" and "act": "A love-play with nine long acts in it / No intervals either!" (59).

Needless to say, translators of a different ideological persuasion avail themselves of the opportunity to make matters clear. Sesar writes, "and spread out nine straight fucks for me," which manages to sound more vulgar than the original because of the added "spread out" combined with the absence of any attempt at wit. Whigham translates:

> [P]repare yourself
> to come nine times
> straight off together.
> (89)

Other more recent translators run variations on the same theme, all using either the noun or the verb quoted above.

Another neologism in Catullus 32 is "lepores" in the second line. Roman readers would normally expect the phrase *amores* in this context: *mei amores*—literally, "my loves" and by implication something like "my beloved." The singular *lepor* means "charm" or "wit." Catullus now substitutes the plural "lepores" for *amores* to emphasize Ipsitilla's charm. With the exception of the Loeb Classical Library translator, who quite rightly translates, "my charmer" (38), none of the translators try to come up with an analog.

Barriss Mills simply recurs to substitution of grammatical categories and translates, "I love you" (62). Aiken cloaks himself in poetic diction and writes, "Soul of my pleasure" (43). Wender opts for a register at the other extreme of the scale and translates, "my cutie" (10). R. A. Swanson stays in the same register with "my doll, kid, baby" (31). Lindsay uses a sociolect that is somewhat dated by now: "you sweet young thing."

Jargon

Catullus 32 also contains an ironic use of military jargon, namely, the adjectival past participle "pransus" in line 10. Its information content is something like "stuffed," "full of food," but it acquires additional illocutionary effect from the cultural fact that the word was used to refer to soldiers after they had been given a hearty meal before an impending battle. Again, the use of precisely this word contributes to the irony content of the original. Only two translators have made an attempt to keep at least something of the military allusion. Raphael and McLeish may be said to have had no other choice, since their whole translation is constructed on the model of a military directive. Accordingly, they render line 10 as "Lying here stiff at attention" (47–48). Wright translates the same line as "I'm ready for the fray" (124), capturing the ironic overtones of the original and at the same time keeping well away from any ideological problems.

Rhyme

Catullus 32 does not rhyme. Yet many translators produce rhyming translations simply because the dominant poetics of their time demands it. There may also be something like an "idiopoetics," an analog on the literary level to what is called idiolect on the level of language. Translators may not necessarily have a poetics entirely of their own making, but they may remain faithful to the poetics that was dominant in the target literature when they were at university or when they first set out to translate and be happily oblivious to any changes that may have occurred in subsequent years.

Rhyming translation almost always results in padding, and sometimes the desperate search for a rhyme word leads translators to the edge of the grotesque, as in Wright's translation of line 9:

> Pray, let me have your answer quick
> And I'll be with you in a tick.   (124)

Both the first and the third line of Lamb and Grainger's translation are not exactly warranted by the original:

> Kind of heart, of beauty bright,
> Pleasure's soul, and love's delight,
> None by nature graced above thee
> Hypsitilla, let me love thee.   (200)

Finally, Aiken renders the third line in the original as five lines in translation:

> . . . Pray do not forget
> to send me grateful information soon

that you're receiving guests this afternoon;
and if, my darling, you will but agree
to save one hour privately for me.   (43)

Word and Thing

A final problem in Catullus 32 is that of the word-thing (or universe-of-discourse) discrepancy centered on "tabellam" in line 5. The word means "panel" of a door that supposedly consists of at least two panels. Only Goold tries to translate accordingly: "that no one locks the panel on your threshold" (73). Other translators either do not worry about the actual shape of Roman doors, or else use Catullus's frame to construct a scene much more indicative of their world than of Catullus's. C. H. Sisson belongs in the first category with the simple "That no one shall get in my way as I enter" (49). Both Burton and Gregory belong in the second category. Forced by rhyme into syntactic contortions, Burton writes, "Undraw thy threshold-bolt none dare," thereby also switching grammatical categories, since the original says something like "let no one put the bolt on the panel of your threshold." Gregory stays much closer to the original but indulges in reverse metonymy by translating, "Let no one bar the door today" (42).

Compensation

Most translators compensate in one way or another: they add features that do not match features in the original on a one-to-one basis but that can be said to be in the spirit of the original. This compensation occurs because translators feel they have not been able to produce the right analog at the right place and therefore add analogs where they are not necessarily warranted to right the balance. When compensating, translators also make use of the devices listed in chapter 2.

Alliteration

Both Goold and Smithers use alliteration to render line 8, probably on the assumption that recurrence to a phonological device will compensate for their inability to supply an analog for "fututiones" on the semantic level. Alliteration is thought to provide a levity analogous to that produced in the reader's mind by the clash of registers on the semantic level in "fututiones." Goold translates, "nine consecutive copulations" (73) in 1983; Smithers has "nine continuous conjoinings" in 1893 (Burton and Smithers), shying away from the word "copulations" in a text addressed to a Victorian audience, even if that text was published "for private subscribers only."

Allusion

Translators also add cultural allusions of their own to establish local color, to give readers the setting they expect to appear in the original even if that setting is not actually there. This tactic is not dissimilar to the one described above under the heading "The Weight of Traditional Interpretations." In this case translators merely exploit the target culture's traditional interpretation of the source culture. The tactic may be designed to reassure readers that they are constructing the right scene on the basis of the frame they have just read in the original. Lamb and Grainger, for instance, insert in their translation a cultural "carpe diem" passage that has no demonstrable analog in the original and that amplifies line 9 into four lines:

> Speed thy message. Day goes fast
> Now's the hour; the banquet's past:
> Midday suns and goblets flowing
> Set my frame with passion glowing.
> (200)

This tactic is by no means limited to older translations, like the one just quoted, which was published in 1854. Aiken, whose translation was published ninety-six years later, inserts a similar "cultural allusion" passage:

> Hasten your summons then, for time runs fast;
> dinner is ended, and the sun is past
> the zenith; garlands fade; the goblet's dry.   (43)

Other translations introduce allusions to the target culture, deliberate anachronisms, inviting readers to construct a scene familiar in the target culture on the basis of the frame that describes an analog in the source culture. Whigham translates "meridiatum" in line 3 as "at siesta" (89); Mills has "the noon siesta" (62). Both suggest a much more languorous afternoon than that indicated by the explicit mention of "nine continuous. . . . "

"Explicitation"

Some translators smuggle what we might call "explicitations" into the text of their translations, probably with the laudable intention of making sure their readers understand what the original is trying to convey. Michie, for instance, translates lines 1 and 2 as:

> Dear Ipsithilla, my sweetheart,
> My darling, precious, beautiful tart.
>   (59)

"Tart" identifies the addressee of the poem as a professional, thus giving readers at one stroke the information Catullus probably intended them to piece together in the process of working their way through the whole text. Moreover, "tart" rhymes with "sweetheart" at the end of the previous line.

Similarly, Smithers translates line 5 quite accurately as "that no one makes fast the outer door" and then adds the somewhat superfluous "against me," ending up with "that no one makes fast the outer door against me." The line makes explicit what readers may already have guessed. Translators tend to smuggle explicitations into their texts mostly because they take very seriously their task as mediators between the original and its new readership. They may feel even more strongly when that original possesses all the prestige of a "classic" of "world literature" and is recognized as such by readers, who expect to be given the "right" access to it.

Off-Rhyme

Where other translations exploited the properties of alliteration to compensate for their lack of semantic inventiveness in rendering the "fututiones" of line 8, Sisson has recourse to off-rhyme. His translation of lines 7 and 8 reads:

> But stay at home and organize for us
> Nine copulations in rapid series.   (49)

His translation, published in 1967, steers a middle course between such Victorian expressions as "conjoinings" and more contemporary *fuck* and *screw* words. His idiolect probably constituted itself in the years before the "sexual revolution" and was not significantly influenced by it.

R. Myers and R. J. Ormsby, by contrast, situate their translation near the core of the sexual revolution by translating the same two lines as "That you will wait for me and choose / To give me nine successive screws" (38), in which the alliterative *s* sounds in the last two words heighten the rhyme. Myers and Ormsby further show that it is possible to use rhyme creatively to reproduce the tone of the original, probably

more convincingly than through the production of semantic illocutionary analogs. Their translation of the first three lines of Catullus 32
reads:

> Ipsithilla, baby girl,
> Sugar, honey, let me curl
> Up with you this afternoon.
> (38)

Gregory uses a distinctive, and by now distinctively dated, sociolect
in his rendition of line 2 as "O mellow, sweet, delicious little piece" (42).
The use of "mellow" as an adjective for a person and "piece" for a de-
lectable person of the female gender establishes the translation as belonging to the mid-fifties to late sixties as clearly as the use of "gender"
in this sentence establishes it as having been written in the nineties.

Word and Thing

Finally, translators tend to exploit the word-thing discrepancy in a creative manner. Nowhere in poem 32 does Catullus say where the speaker
is lying, but the reader is probably meant to infer that he is lying in bed
after breakfast. Whigham has the speaker "lolling on / the sofa here"
(10), inviting readers to construct a scene that corresponds to the altered
frame. When the new scene is projected back into the cultural context of
the original, it becomes incongruous, but its very incongruity forces
readers to hark back to the human universal underlying the culturally
determined situation described in Catullus 32.

Conclusion

The preceding pages are intended to provide an object lesson for the
analysis of a whole translated text, as opposed to the analysis of translated chunks of text described in chapter 1. In what follows I try to describe the various stages of that analysis in a more abstract and therefore
more easily transposable way, for it must be evident by now that an analysis of a translated text can serve at least two purposes. First, it can show
aspiring translators how their predecessors have tried to cope with the
problems presented by a text. Second, it can show how the global strategy translators develop, combined with the many tactical decisions based
on that strategy, can create a certain image of the original in the target
culture. That image can sometimes be relatively far removed from the

reality presented by the source text. The important point here, though, is that the difference between image and reality simply does not matter, does not even exist, for those readers who cannot compare the source text with its translation. Since those readers constitute the great majority of the readers of translations, they may find themselves at the mercy of translators who wish to project a particular image of the original for ideological or poetological reasons or both. This possibility explains much of the distrust with which translation and translators have been regarded in the past; it also explains why translators can wield a certain power—and have done so throughout history—and why the images they create may become influential in the development of literatures. We shall deal with these problems in more detail in chapter 4.

Beyond "Mistake Spotting"

The first stage in analyzing a translation is a negative one: analysts need to suppress the knee-jerk impulse to label any slight or obvious deviation from the source text as a "mistake." Rather, they should ascertain whether there is a pattern to the deviations. Here is a possible rule of thumb: Isolated deviations are mistakes; deviations that can be shown to follow certain patterns indicate a strategy the translator has developed to deal with the text as a whole.

Reconstruction of Translation Strategies

Translators develop their global strategy on the basis of answers they give to the following questions, listed here in hierarchical order:

1. Can the original be made to fit in with the dominant ideology of the target culture at the time the translation is made? If so, there is no problem at all. Translators may proceed with the translation in the confident expectation that it will eventually be published. If the translation is commissioned by a publisher, that publisher has answered question 1 for the translator.

2. If the answer to 1 is no, translators may proceed to ask whether there is a sufficiently strong peripheral ideological current in the target culture that may have a need, or a use, for a translation of a text that challenges the dominant ideology. Could the translation, in other words, be used as an ally in the struggle against the dominant ideology? If so, the translation has a fair chance of being published and at least partially accepted. The translation may even help develop the target culture by

introducing a model, or one of a number of possible models, that may serve as a catalyst for peripheral ideological currents.

If the answer to both questions 1 and 2 is no, translators would be well advised not to translate the work in question but to leave that task to future generations. In practice most translators have at least one "impossible" pet project that they embark on against their better judgment, simply because they cannot resist a certain text and need to try to translate it, regardless of the odds against publication.

To certain timeless classics, among them Catullus, questions 1 and 2 do not apply. Although these texts tend to fall in and out of ideological favor over time (witness the deletions and euphemisms in the translations analyzed), as classics they are assured of a permanent audience.

3. Can the text be easily assimilated into an existing text type in the target culture? Assimilation is not likely to be a problem if the translation is done from one Western language into another. It might be quite a problem if the translation needs to be done from a Western into a non-Western language or vice versa. In that case translators have to move on to the next question:

4. Might the original be convincingly turned into a variant of a text type established in the target literature? If this is possible, the translation stands a fair chance of succeeding; if not, translators have to move on to yet another question.

5. Can the label the author of the original bears in his or her own culture (mellifluous Catullus, for instance, or erotic Sappho) be made to match the label of an author in the target culture? If so, transfer may occur based on this analog, and this type of transfer may override the problem of text type. Translators might state in their introduction that the source-text writer X "reads very like" the target-culture writer Y and that readers should bear the similarity in mind as they proceed through the unfamiliar text type. In fact, matching labels might well prove to be a handy strategy for introducing new text types or genres into the target literature.

We have already remarked that translators can translate with or against the label a given author carries. Since that label is always reductionist, translators may opt to reveal hidden sides of the original author by simply translating against the label. More generally, translators may have to answer the next question in an analogous fashion.

6. Is it possible, or even likely, that a translation of the text under consideration might serve as a model or catalyst for peripheral countercurrents to the dominant poetics of the target literature and that it could play a part in the struggle between two or more rival poetics?

   Translators should be able to relate tactical decisions made on the universe-of-discourse level and on the level of illocutionary language use to the strategy devised in response to the questions listed above. If they cannot, the decisions are mistakes, reflecting the failures of the translators to properly understand the source text.

Implications

This type of analysis dramatically reveals that translators need a wide and deep knowledge of both source and target literatures. Literary scholars are more likely to possess this knowledge than creative writers or "gifted amateurs" are. Ironically, though, as we have seen, when literary scholars use that knowledge in the production of translations, they risk having their work discounted as inferior to such incrementally less obvious forms of rewriting as criticism and historiography.

   For translation students this type of analysis can profitably be repeated over and over again. It is advisable to let students select classical poems from their native literatures, since those are likely to have spawned the most translations over the years. They should each produce an interlinear translation, supplement it with both a "literal" translation and a commentary, and analyze different translations following the model outlined above. In class discussions students should be encouraged to propose possible translation strategies and possible translations of the tactical problems explained by their classmates. Not infrequently this type of analysis is conducive to the production of quite acceptable translations by student translators who have no knowledge of either the language of the source text or the literature of the source culture. Finally, the type of analysis exemplified here can be expanded into a more extensive research project.

Works Cited

Aiken, W. A., trans. *The Poems of Catullus*. New York: Dutton, 1950.

Burton, Sir Richard, and L. C. Smithers, trans. *The Carmina of Caius Valerius Catullus*. London: privately printed, 1893. N. pag.

Catullus. Tibullus. Pervigilium Veneris. Trans. F. W. Cornish. Loeb Classical Library. London: Heinemann; Cambridge: Harvard UP, 1968.

Copley, F. O., trans. *Gaius Valerius Catullus: The Complete Poetry*. Ann Arbor: U of Michigan P, 1957.

Fillmore, Charles J. "Scenes-and-Frames Semantics." *Linguistic Structures Processing*. Ed. A. Zampolli. Amsterdam: North Holland, 1977. 55–81.

Goold, G. P., trans. *Catullus*. London: Duckworth, 1983.

Gregory, Horace. *The Poems of Catullus*. New York: Grove, 1956.

Kelly, W., trans. *Erotica: The Poems of Catullus and Tibullus*. London: Bohn, 1854.

Lindsay, Jack, trans. *Catullus: The Complete Poems*. London: Sylvan, 1948. N. pag.

Michie, James, trans. *The Poems of Catullus*. New York: Random, 1969.

Mills, Barriss, trans. *The Carmina of Catullus*. Lafayette: Purdue U Studies, 1965.

Myers, R., and R. J. Ormsby, trans. *Catullus: The Complete Poems for American Readers*. New York: Dutton, 1970.

Raphael, Frederic, and K. McLeish, trans. *The Poems of Catullus*. London: Cape, 1978.

Sesar, C., trans. *Selected Poems of Catullus*. New York: Mason, 1974. N. pag.

Sisson, C. H., trans. *The Poetry of Catullus*. New York: Orion, 1967.

Swanson, R. A., trans. *Odi et Amo*. New York: Liberal Arts, 1959.

Vannerem, Mia, and Mary Snell-Hornby. "Die Szene hinter dem Text: 'Scenes-and-Frames Semantics' in der Übersetzung." *Übersetzungswissenschaft—Eine Neuorientierung*. Ed. Mary Snell-Hornby. Tübingen: Francke, 1986. 184–205.

Wender, Dorothea, ed. and trans. *Roman Poetry*. Carbondale: Southern Illinois UP, 1980.

Whigham, Peter, trans. *The Poems of Catullus*. Harmondsworth, Eng.: Penguin, 1966.

Wright, F. A., trans. *Catullus*. London: Routledge; New York: Dutton, n.d.

Zukofsky, Louis, and Celia Zukofsky, trans. *Catullus*. London: Cape Goliard, 1969. N. pag.

Chapter 4
Context:
The Function of Translation in a Culture

From Text to Context:
Categories for Further Analysis

The last part of this book looks at how translations function within the wider context of a literature and, by extension, a culture. Again, suggestions for research are given in a somewhat schematized manner and supplemented by somewhat schematized examples. The chapter is sprinkled with quotations taken only from the writings of pre-nineteenth-century writers on translation, not only to dispel the notion that the ideas expressed are novel but also to reveal the existence of a long tradition of writing on translation in the West.

Probably the first translation produced in the West was the translation of the Old Testament known as the Septuagint. Legend has it that the translation was produced by seventy (seventy-two in some variants) translators, each working in a separate cell. They all translated the whole text, and all translations miraculously turned out to be identical. The translators were sent to Alexandria by Eleazar, high priest of Jerusalem, at the request of Ptolemy II, king of Egypt. Made for the benefit of those Jewish communities in Egypt who could no longer read the original, the translation became the basis for later translations into Old Latin, Coptic, Armenian, Georgian, and Slavonic.

The legend provides us with the main categories we need to analyze the part translations play in a culture. Translation involves expertise: since the seventy or seventy-two translators all produced the same target text, they must have known their trade. Their knowledge was guaranteed and probably checked by some authority beyond their immediate group. That instance can only have been supernatural in the legend since the story holds that the translators were inspired by the Holy Ghost. Beyond the domain of legend, the person checking a translation turns out to be extremely human indeed. There is little that is "holy" about experts checking and finally arriving at some sort of consensus.

Translation also involves commission: a person in authority orders the translation to be made. Translation fills, or is thought to fill, a need: the Jewish communities in Egypt were able to read the Old Testament again. Finally, translation involves trust: the intended readers who do not know the original trust that the translation is a fair representation of that original. The readers trust the experts and, by implication, those who check on the experts.

As it happened, that trust was misplaced by readers of the Septuagint. Various versions were found to differ greatly from one another, and later versions became so "christianized" that the Jewish communities stopped using the translation altogether. Yet the fact that the Septuagint was a "bad" translation did nothing to undermine its image. On the contrary, it served as the basis for translations into many other languages of the ancient Mediterranean world, and it is used by the Greek Church to this day.

These, then, are the categories for translation analysis that goes beyond individual texts: first, authority—not only the authority of the patron, the person or institution commissioning or publishing the translation, but also the authority of a culture viewed as the central culture in a given time or a geographical area and the authority of the text; second, expertise, checked and guaranteed; and, third, trust, the kind of trust that survives bad translations.

To these categories we must add two more: the image of the source text a translator consciously or unconsciously sets out to develop and the readers, the intended audience.

Audience

Different audiences need translations for different reasons. Children, as we saw in chapter 2, do not need the same translations as adults. But different groups of adults also need different translations. Between 500 and 1600 the audience for European literary culture was not only relatively small but also basically bilingual or even multilingual. European intellectuals shared a generally respected "language of authority": first Latin, then French, known by all those professing to be ecclesiastics, scholars, or literati. They would know their native tongues as well and often one additional language or more. It would not be unusual for four writers to meet over beer or, in a later age, coffee and for two of them to go home and write in their native tongues while the other two would write in Latin or, later, French.

Strange as it may seem to us, readers of that time read translations not because they could not read the originals but because they wanted to compare the translations with the originals. They produced translations as exercises, first as exercises in school, to learn foreign languages and to perfect their style in their own languages, and later as exercises in appropriating foreign texts to usurp the authority of those texts, to prove that the language and culture of the reader were as good as the language and culture of the original.

Once the sphere of culture began to encompass more and more people who knew fewer and fewer languages, translations began to be read more for their information content; they were no longer just valued for the proof they represented of the illocutionary power of a language or a certain translator or group of translators, even though the best translations were thought—and are still thought today—to be those that combine the maximum of both. And once readers began to read translations for information, it followed that different translations had to be made for different groups or with different goals in mind. In Goethe's words, "If you want to influence the masses, a simple translation is always best. Critical translations vying with the original really are of use only for conversations the learned conduct among themselves" (38). As soon as different translations had to be made for different groups, it became plainly impossible to formulate any but the most trivial rules for the production of translation without taking into account the potential audience.

Authority

Patrons

Authority draws the ideological parameters of the acceptable. It influences (sometimes outright dictates) the selection of texts for translating as well as the ways in which those texts are to be translated. In John of Trevisa's fifteenth-century "Dialogue between a Lord and a Clerk upon Translation," the Lord makes it clear that he is paying the piper and expects to call the tune. He says, "I desire not translation of these the best that might be, for that were an idle desire for any man that is now alive, but I would have a skillful translation, that might be known and understood." He wants a translation that is effective, that is intelligible to the intended audience, and he is discussing the translation not of literature but of moral texts. The Clerk just wants to make sure and asks, "Whether is you liefer have, a translation of these chronicles in rhyme or prose?" Again the answer is refreshingly blunt: "In prose, for commonly prose is more clear than rhyme, more easy and more plain to know and understand."

Had he been commissioning a translation of Vergil's *Aeneid,* the Lord would not have suggested that it be done in prose. But there was no point in translating Vergil for the audience the Lord had in mind: his tenants, whose general manners and behavior he wanted to improve. He was not interested in subsidizing a translation (of the *Aeneid*, for instance) that would have served only "for conversations the learned conduct among themselves." Fortunately, other lords were prepared to subsidize such translations.

Translators know who pays the piper and give advice to other translators accordingly. In a little-quoted passage from his best-known work, Joachim Du Bellay ends his admonitions to translators with the following revealing sentence: "[W]hat I say is not meant for those who, at the command of princes and great lords, translate the most famous Greek and Latin writers since the obedience one owes to those persons admits of no excuse in these matters" (52).

About a hundred years later the earl of Roscommon refers to patrons of a different kind and the way they treat translators:

> I pity from my Soul unhappy Men
> Compelled by Want to prostitute their Pen
> Who must, like Lawyers, either starve or plead
> And follow, right or wrong, where Guineas lead.
>   (82)

Around 1700, with the growth of literacy and the gradual spread of a more open type of society, the authorities were no longer just "princes and great lords"; they were joined by publishers, who started commissioning translations of books that sold well in other countries. Publishers paid their translators poorly, contributing to, if not actually causing, the translators' loss of social and intellectual status. As publishers became more powerful in deciding what was going to be translated and how, the ideological parameters set for translators began to widen, since publishers' decisions were chiefly based on profit.

When translators were commissioned to translate a given work of literature, most often because of that work's success in another country, they increasingly tended to screen out those ideological and universe-of-discourse features of the original they believed would not be acceptable to their intended audience. They did so from a well-conceived sense of their own advantage: if they translated what was likely to offend the audience, the translation was not likely to sell, the publisher was likely to lose money and therefore most unlikely to offer the translator another commission. Still, from the translator's point of view, this situation was a great improvement over the one a few centuries before, when those in authority could, and did, burn translators at the stake for not translating the Bible "right."

Whether an audience is reading the Bible or other works of literature, it often wants to see its own ideology and its own universe of discourse mirrored in the translation. It likes to re-create the world in its own image, sometimes with startling results, as in Abbé Prévost's translation of Samuel Richardson's *Pamela*. Prévost writes in his introduction:

> I have suppressed English customs where they may appear shocking to other nations, or else made them conform to customs prevalent in the rest of Europe. It seemed to me that those remainders of the old and uncouth British ways, which only habit prevents the British themselves from noticing, would dishonor a book in which manners should be noble and virtuous. To give the reader an accurate idea of my work, let me just say, in conclusion, that the seven volumes of the English edition, which would amount to fourteen volumes in my own, have been reduced to four.   (trans. mine)

Obviously the good Abbé was not in the habit of providing "faithful" translations; more important, he never even thought it might be a good idea to try. Since the manners of his, the target, culture were superior to those of the source culture, it was axiomatic to him that the "bad" manners should not be allowed to influence the "good" ones.

Cultures

At certain times certain cultures are considered more prestigious, more "authoritative" than other, neighboring cultures or successor cultures. A culture will be perceived as central by another if the perceiving culture believes it has much to learn from the other. The central position a culture occupies is therefore a matter of comparative cultural prestige. French culture was central for Germany during the first half of the eighteenth century. The culture of classical antiquity has been central to Europe from the Renaissance to our century. The culture of T'ang China has been central to Japan during certain historical periods.

In the European Middle Ages this situation gave rise to the (to us) strange phenomenon of "reverse translation." Since the learned were bilingual anyway and since the prestige of Latin eclipsed that of any other language except classical Greek, there was little need for translation and few translations were produced. Since it was hard to be taken seriously as a scholar in the arts or the sciences (the two were then much more closely connected) if one did not write at least partly in Latin, many literati did, partaking of the authority of that language. Yet what many readers may be tempted to think of as strange and confined to the Dark Ages is happening in our own time as well: many writers and intellectuals living in former colonies tend to write at least part of their work in the former "language of authority," the language of the colonizer. Many of them, moreover, live all their lives without ever communicating with families and friends in their native tongues.

A touching and amusing case of reverse translation in the Middle Ages is also attested in the popular literature, particularly in folk songs. These were often anonymous productions written by persons with little education. Yet to show that they, too, should be taken seriously, the authors would sprinkle their songs with what Latin phrases they knew, usually phrases like "Deo gratias" (thanks be to God) and other responsories from the Mass, the only Latin "text" to which they were regularly exposed.

Members of "superior" cultures tend to look down on members of "inferior" cultures and to treat cavalierly the literature of those cultures. The relation between superior and inferior cultures does not necessarily remain the same over the centuries. In the sixteenth and early seventeenth century the French attitude toward Homer, for instance, was very different from that described by Johann Gottfried Herder in the eighteenth century:

> The French, who are overproud of their natural taste, adapt all things to it, rather than try to adapt themselves to the taste of another time. Homer must enter France a captive, and dress according to fashion, so as not to offend their eyes. He has to allow them to take his venerable beard and his old simple clothes away from him. He has to conform to the French customs, and where his peasant coarseness still shows he is ridiculed as a barbarian. (31)

French translators did to Homer what Abbé Prévost did to Richardson's *Pamela*. Yet the French were by no means the only ones to indulge in this kind of behavior. About a hundred years later, Edward FitzGerald, the famous translator of the *Rubáiyát of Omar Khayyám* and a representative of the "next" superior culture, that of Victorian England, wrote to his friend E. B. Cowell, "It is an amusement for me to take what Liberties I like with these Persians who (as I think) are not Poets enough to frighten one from such excursions, and who really do want a little Art to shape them" (xvi). FitzGerald would never have taken the same liberties with classical Greek or Roman authors, not only because they represented a superior culture but also because there were too many experts around who could check his translation.

The attitude that uses one's own culture as the yardstick by which to measure all other cultures is known as ethnocentricity. I submit that all cultures have it but that only those who achieve some kind of superiority flaunt it. Cultures that do not flaunt it would if they could, but since they cannot they pretend to be free of it. An ethnocentric attitude allows members of a culture to remake the world in their image, without first having to realize how different the reality of that world is. It produces translations that are tailored to the target culture exclusively and that screen out whatever does not fit in with it.

An obstreperous variant of ethnocentrism, potentially more obnoxious because harder to pin down, is known in translation studies as Eurocentrism. It holds that only the study of European or European-based cultures is feasible. But it never explicitly asserts this view. Instead, it "changes grammatical categories," so to speak, energetically lamenting the difficulties of studying non-European cultures, let alone translating into them, while being inwardly glad that these difficulties do indeed exist. Eurocentrists are not European supremacists in any way; they just believe that the study of and translation from and into non-European cultures should not be encouraged, even though they pay lip service to it. This attitude is responsible for the woefully inadequate research conducted into problems of translation that arise outside the charmed circle of Europe and its historical dependencies.

Texts

Cultures that derive their ultimate authority from a text—be it the Bible, the Qur'an, or *The Communist Manifesto*—are likely to guard that text with special vigilance, since the power of those empowered can be said to rest on it. Accordingly, translators of such texts are allowed little leeway, as certain medieval and Renaissance European Bible translators who ended their days at the stake learned to their dismay.

Some sacred central texts like the Qur'an are not allowed to be translated at all. Or, rather, true believers are not allowed to translate it. Yet the Qur'an has exercised a pervasive influence on world history, an influence that goes beyond its own historical dominance. Nontranslation of the Qur'an persists not because there are no Muslims capable of translating the work into other languages but simply because the authorities desire to protect their authority.

Even though the Bible has often been translated, it has been translated in a special way for a long time. The reason for this special treatment is eloquently stated by Petrus Danielus Huetius, one of the most important writers on translation, but one of the ones least remembered, probably because his work, written in Latin, was never translated. Huetius writes:

> I insist on treating Holy Writ with such diligence and care because I do not want the oracles of the Holy Ghost to be adulterated by human and earth-bound elements. For it is not without divine counsel that they have been expressed in certain selected words, selected from a certain sphere and arranged in a certain order, for there are as many mysteries hidden in them as there are dots in the text. And did not Christ himself say that not one dot should be erased from the Law until heaven and earth are destroyed?
>
> (23; trans. mine)

Such faithful, even literal, translation is reserved for books that are repositories of a culture's central authority. Yet by analogy this kind of translation can be extended to works considered classics of world literature. It happens not infrequently that a certain translation, the first translation of such a classic to be made into a certain language, remains an authoritative text, even lives on as an authoritative text in its own right long after it has ceased to function as a translation. Jacques Amyot's translation of Plutarch into French is such a classic of translation, as are John Harington's translation of Ariosto into English and the so-called Tieck-Schlegel translation (the real translators of most of it were Ludwig Tieck's sister Dorothea and Count Baudissin) of Shakespeare into German.

Such authoritative texts/translations tend to acquire a timeless quality of their own, and readers do not easily part with them. They come to trust the translator if for no other reason than that the translation is the one they are familiar with. Readers often feel reluctant to switch to another, newer translation, even if experts have pronounced it better. This reflex is most pronounced regarding a culture's central texts and explains the dogged survival of bad translations—like the Septuagint. It underlies musings like the following, excerpted from Auden's "Doggerel by a Senior Citizen":

The Book of Common Prayer we knew
Was that of 1662:

Though with-it sermons may be well,
Liturgical reforms are hell.
(Amis 271)

Authority Usurped

Translations share in the authority of the text they represent. One might say that translations usurp to some extent the authority of their source texts. After all, if you have something to say, why not say it in your own right instead of translating it. The answer may be not that you lack inspiration or artistic ability but that you believe what you have to say may carry more weight if you say it in someone else's name.

Perhaps the most glaring example of this cultural strategy is the so-called pseudotranslation: a text that purports to be a translation but is not. Many "translations" of the works of nonexistent English philosophers appeared in eighteenth-century France, because England was known for its advanced political views and envied for its more constitutional form of government. Political writers who wanted to influence public opinion in the direction of reform or revolution felt that their words would carry more weight if they could be put in the mouth of a "philosopher" from a country that had already undergone a "glorious revolution" and emerged the better for it. Pseudotranslations can therefore play a not insignificant part in the struggle between rival political philosophies.

They can also play an important part in the struggle between rival poetics. James McPherson's *Ossian* comes to mind in the struggle between Augustan and pre-Romantic poetics in English literature, as do Thomas Chatterton's medieval pastiches and Thomas Percy's *Reliques*. The rationale behind this strategy is clearly described by Horace Walpole in the two prefaces to his novel *The Castle of Otranto*, which was to become the model for a new genre, the gothic novel. In the first preface Walpole represents the novel as a translation of an Italian manuscript. He even promises to "reprint the original Italian" in case the novel "should meet with success" (41). In the second preface, written after the novel has indeed met with success, Walpole apologizes: "it is fit that he [the author] should ask pardon of his readers for having offered his work to them under the borrowed personage of a translator" (43). His excuse for having done so lies in "the novelty of the attempt . . . to blend the two kinds of romance, the ancient and the modern" (43). In other words, Walpole did not feel inclined to mount a frontal—and probably doomed—attack on the dominant poetics of his time. Rather, he wanted to experiment with an alternative poetics under the cover of translation, revealing the truth only when he thought the experiment succeeded.

Authority Bestowed

Translation usurps authority but it also bestows authority. It bestows authority on a language. In Cicero's words:

> [B]y giving a Latin form to the text I had read I could not only make use of the best expressions in common usage with us but I could also coin new expressions analogous to those used in Greek and they were no less well received by our people, as long as they seemed appropriate. (147)

Translation forces a language to expand, and that expansion may be welcome as long as it is checked by the linguistic community at large.

Translation can also bestow the authority inherent in a language of authority (Latin, French, English, Russian) on a text originally written in another language lacking that authority. Many works of literature written in "minor" languages, such as August Strindberg's plays, might not now belong to the canon of world literature if they had not originally been launched in a language of authority—French, in this case. Similarly, Ibsen's plays were introduced to Europe not in his native Norwegian but in German by the Berlin People's Theater.

The pervasive influence of translation is so great that these works written in other languages cease, after a while, to be thought of as "foreign" to the language of authority. English departments routinely teach Ibsen and Strindberg, and the only feature that alerts students to the fact that they are reading translations may be a difficulty in pronouncing the names of the characters.

Conversely, speakers of emerging languages tend to want to translate works of literature written in languages of authority simply to prove that their languages are equally expressive. As pointed out before, the process can be observed on a large scale in the European Renaissance, and it can be observed again in nineteenth-century Europe, particularly Eastern Europe, where a number of languages want to be recognized as full-fledged members of the European intellectual, literary, and artistic community. It can also be seen in our time in those parts of the world colonized between the end of the eighteenth and the middle of the twentieth century. Writers and intellectuals translate the great writings produced by the culture of their former colonial overlords. Julius Nyerere, for instance, translated Shakespeare into Swahili not because such a translation was needed to convey information but because he wished to prove that Swahili could do all the things Shakespeare could do in English, that Swahili was a worthy instrument waiting for a genius to play it.

Translation also allows writers in the target culture to proceed on the authority of writers alien to the target literature and introduced into it by translators. In other words, translation introduces new devices into the literatures by which it is received. The sonnet was introduced into Chinese literature through Feng Chi's translations published in the 1920s. The ode became the major genre for writers of the Pléiade after it had been translated extensively into French from Greek and Latin. Under the moralizing aegis of the Jesuits, translation transformed the picaresque novel into the German bildungsroman. The alternation of masculine and feminine rhymes in French goes back to Octavien de St. Gelais's translations of Ovid. The hexameter was introduced into German poetry through the Homer translations of Johann Heinrich Voss. John Hookham Frere's translations of Luigi Pulci reintroduced ottava rima into English literature, where it was soon picked up by Byron and masterfully used in *Don Juan*. Yet Goethe's pious "hope that literary history will plainly state who was the first to take this road in spite of so many obstacles" (39) tends to remain exactly that. Literary histories have until now had little time for translations, since for the literary historian translation has been a matter of language only, not of literature. This attitude is a pernicious outgrowth of the "monolingualization" of literary history introduced by Romantic historiographers and perpetuated by their disciples, both intent on creating "national" literatures preferably as uncontaminated by "foreign" influences as possible.

Only recently have literary histories begun to acknowledge the part played by translation in the evolution of a literature. David Perkins writes in his *History of Modern Poetry*:

> Just how or when the Celtic Movement began is a matter of dispute. Yeats's *The Wanderings of Oisin* (1899) is sometimes taken as the inaugural production. But in this poem Yeats is dependent on the work of Sir Samuel Ferguson who in *Lays of the Western Gael* (1865), *Congal* (1872), *Deirdre* (1880) and *Poems* (1880) had gone back to the ancient Irish legends—which Yeats could not read in the original—and had rendered them into English verse.   (26)

Only recently, too, have monographs on individual writers begun to acknowledge how translations have influenced authors. Byron, for instance, "made it clear" in his *Don Juan* that *"De l'Allemagne* was the obvious source for the average littérateur's knowledge of Goethe" (Martin 125); Byron was referring to the forty-five pages Mme de Staël devoted to *Faust* in her book. Those forty-five pages consist of translated extracts and paraphrases. If the average British writer knew neither French nor German, he or she would have to make do with a severely truncated paraphrase of *Faust,* including a few translated passages, published in Maurice Retzsch's *Outlines.* The first complete English translation of *Faust* appeared in 1835, three years after the death of Byron, who, all biographers agree, was greatly influenced by Goethe's most famous work.

Image: Culture

Preserving the Self-Image of the Target Culture

Translations not only project an image of the work that is translated and, through it, of the world that work belongs to; they also protect their own world against images that are too radically different, either by adapting them or by screening them out. Victor Hugo writes about a culture's negative reaction to translation:

> To translate a foreign poet is to add to one's own poetry; yet this addition does not please those who profit from it. At least not in the beginning: the first reaction is one of revolt. A language into which another idiom is transfused does what it can to resist. It will find new strength in it later, but for now it is indignant. It abhors that new taste. (iii–iv; trans. mine)

It is a sobering thought that China hardly seems to have translated anything after the great wave of translating the Buddhist scriptures in the eighth century. Significant translation activity was resumed only about ten centuries later when the Western powers forced the Chinese to open a channel to them.

Changing the Self-Image of the Target Culture

Some translations have significantly changed the image the target culture had of itself. Perhaps the most far-reaching change was made on

the basis of a simple shift in grammatical categories. The Aramaic the
historical Jesus spoke has no copula, that is, it does not express the verb
to be. That verb appears for the first time in the Greek translation, and
theologians have not stopped arguing over its true meaning since, burn-
ing each other at the stake and starting more than a few holy conflicts
along the way as long as they had the power to do so.

It is worth noting in this context that a translation of the Bible made
by a defrocked Augustinian monk contributed mightily to changing the
face of Europe in his time and for ever after. Yet he was very aware that
the quality of his translation was but one factor, and not the primary
one, among many contributing to its importance. In the following extract from his *Table Talk* Martin Luther not only laments the pirating of
his translation by "the scribbler in Dresden"; he also realizes that his
translation is being used as a weapon in the struggle between two op-
posing ideologies:

> We are aware of the scribbler in Dresden who stole my New Tes-
> tament. He admitted that my German is good and sweet and he
> realized that he could not do better and yet he wanted to discredit
> it, so he took my New Testament as I wrote it, almost word for
> word, and he took my preface, my glosses and my name away and
> wrote his name, his preface and his glosses in their place. He is now
> selling my New Testament under his name. Oh, dear children, how
> hurt I was when his prince, in a terrible preface, forbade the read-
> ing of Luther's New Testament but ordered the scribbler's New
> Testament read, which is exactly the same as the one Luther
> wrote.   (8)

Some words that have gone on to play a significant part in the target
culture "started out" as translations. When the early Christians had to
translate into Latin the word *mysterion* from the Greek texts of the Bible,
they did not simply Latinize, or "calque," it, because a mere calque
would have come too close to the vocabulary used by the mystery cults
competing with Christianity at the time. Latin equivalents such as *sacra,
arcana,* or *initia* were felt to be somewhat uncomfortably obvious, for the
same ideological reasons. As a result, the third-century translator of the
oldest Latin version of the Bible came up with the word *sacramentum,*
which must have seemed both ideologically neutral and an acceptable
analog. When Jerome wrote his translation of the Bible, the so-called
Vulgate, he felt free to Latinize the Greek *mysterion* because the pagan
mystery cults had ceased to be a threat to the Christian church. Yet the

word *sacramentum* went on to a great future in most European languages, even though, or precisely because, it no longer functioned as a translation (cf. Klopsch 137–38).

Acculturation

On the level of universe of discourse the clash between two cultures can result in various forms of misunderstanding, of acculturation, and all kinds of mixtures in between. When Joseph D. Carlyle, an early English Arabist, tried to translate Labid's qasidah, one of the seven pre-Islamic canonized works of Arabic literature, he came across the word *diman* 'dung heap' and omitted it altogether from his translation. The reference in the original is to camel dung, which is to be found in the desert and is not to be spurned, because it can be used as fuel. Yet it is hardly what a Victorian translator would regard as proper and definitely not as poetic. German translators did translate the word but for the wrong universe-of-discourse reasons. Since they were "familiar with the peasants of their own land, where the size of the dung heap is some indication of the prosperity of the farmer, [they] merely transposed to the desert the social values of Bavaria" (Polk xxviii). The reader is invited to picture huge dung heaps arising mysteriously in the middle of the desert rather than isolated camel droppings.

Good or ill fortune may therefore befall a translation as the result of a translator's understanding or misunderstanding of the original's universe of discourse. Problems also arise, however, when the translator is fully aware of that universe of discourse. A simple transliteration of the wu t'ung tree, a rather ordinary tree in China, achieves an exotic effect. If, however, translators turn the wu t'ung tree into a tree familiar to readers in the target culture, they naturalize what is, in effect, foreign. Here one might ask how a translator's strategy is affected by the extent to which the foreign culture is seen as central to the development of the target culture. On the whole, translators more painstakingly retain universe-of-discourse features belonging to a culture they consider central. Some may decide to retain the exotic flavor at all costs if the exotic has a special flavor in their own universe of discourse.

In practice the problem of acculturation tends to solve itself as cultural environments grow closer together. This process is often slower where isolationist or politically less influential cultures are involved. Primarily a cumulative process, it has to go through the explanatory phase until what is explained becomes part of the conceptual environment of the target culture. The first translators of Russian literature into

Western European languages would explain in a footnote what kind of soup borscht was; not quite a hundred years later that soup is served in many restaurants in Western Europe.

Challenging a Poetics

Cultures may resist translation because it is felt to threaten their self-image. Poetics may resist translation for the same reason. In fact, translation provides probably the best way to gauge the influence of a poetics at a certain time in history since it shows the degree to which translators have interiorized that poetics, the degree to which it has become "self-evident" to them. The following quotation is a somewhat extreme example, but it must be stressed that the translator does not act out of any conscious desire to mutilate or otherwise degrade the source text. Rather he is convinced of the self-evidence of his own poetics, to the extent that he cannot even conceive of the existence of an alternative. He is convinced that what he has done was not just the right but the only thing to do and that he has done the original a favor by ruthlessly adapting it to the poetics of the target literature:

> I have reduced the twenty-four books of the *Iliad* to twelve, which are even shorter than Homer's. At first sight you might think that this could only be done at the expense of many important features; but if you pause to reflect that repetitions make up more than one sixth of the *Iliad* and that the anatomical details of wounds and the long speeches of the fighters make up a lot more, you will be right in thinking that it has been easy for me to shorten the poem without losing any important features of the plot. I flatter myself with the thought that I have done just that, and I even think I have brought together the essential parts of the action in such a way that they are shaped into a whole better proportioned and more sensible in my abbreviated version than in the original.
>
> (Motte 17; trans. mine)

Needless to say, this attitude is fostered by the translator's conviction of the central position, the superiority, of his own culture.

Translations play an important part in the struggle between rival poetics. The basic pattern is usually the same: dissatisfaction with the dominant poetics takes the form of (often ringing) manifestos or declarations of intent drawn up by writers subscribing to a new poetics and aimed at subverting the dominant poetics. The very fact that the new

poetics is new is likely to lead to the embarrassing situation in which
"new" writers have little more than a blueprint to oppose to the solid
body of work produced (admittedly over a number of decades or centuries) in the established poetics.

In the struggle for the allegiance of the reading public, the established poetics can point to prestigious finished products whereas the
adherents of the new poetics cannot yet do so. Consequently the chal-
lengers begin to import their own "finished products": translations of
writers who are as prestigious in their own literature as the adherents of
the established poetics in the target literature. These foreign writers
"happen" to have produced work that fits in wonderfully well with the
new poetics, or they can be shown to have done so, even if they themselves were not aware of their role as "precursors." Hence not only Ezra
Pound's ruthless "imagization" of classical Chinese poetry but also the
countless translations made by the imagists of the triad Sappho, Catullus,
Villon. That the products displayed by the adherents of the new poetics
are imported from prestigious foreign systems helps to brand the dominant poetics and its adherents as more or less hopelessly provincial.

Imported products also tend to possess a certain immunity inside
the target culture because they are situated on the borderline between
the "native" (and therefore subject to the full wrath of the dominant poetics) and the "foreign" (and therefore relatively exempt from the rules
of the dominant poetics). This ambiguous status allows translations to
embark on a course of subversion by infiltration.

Finally, poetics tends to be the level where the effective translatability or untranslatability of the source text is decided. The qasidah, for instance, the most prestigious genre of Arabic poetry, derives its unity not
from plot or argumentation, as do longer poems produced in the West,
but from its treatment of certain themes in a certain sequence, no matter at what length. The overall length of the poem is also immaterial.
The qasidah has to begin with the thematic component in which the
poet and his friends ride through the desert. He spots the remains of a
former campsite and begins to weep because the place reminds him of
past happiness. Other necessary thematic components are the evocation
of that lost happiness, the poet's love for a woman, praise for the poet's
prowess as a poet and a lover, praise for the poet's patron, and, finally,
a description of nature.

The classical genre of Arabic poetry looks totally out of place in
Western poetics. Early Western Arabists trained in the poetics of Western literatures tried to find the nearest acceptable equivalent in their
own poetics. They came up with the (mostly Pindaric) ode in French,

German, and English. The result failed to meet the expectations with which Western readers approached the ode, and consequently the qasidah failed to become integrated in the Western system to the extent to which translations of Chinese and Japanese lyrical poetry did. The latter translations could be made to fit the Western reader's idea of the lyric.

Expertise and Trust

Patrons commission translations and publish them. They do not check them. They leave that task to experts employed to check one another's expertise. This checking process takes place most obviously in the pedagogical situation. As late as the mid–seventeenth century Johann Christoph Gottsched states in his *Ausführliche Redekunst* (Comprehensive Art of Oratory) that translation is "precisely what the copying of a given model is to a beginner in the art of painting. We know that the works of the great masters are copied with pleasure and diligence by mediocre artists or by beginners who would like to make their way" (15). The experts also delimit the poetological parameters of the translation: Will the finished product be acceptable as literature in the target culture? Will it conform to the poetics currently dominating that culture?

Experts have always been aware of the problems we have touched on in this book, even though they sometimes call them by different names. Jean le Rond d'Alembert, for instance, has this to say about adaptation of the source text for ideological reasons:

> We transfer the classics into our own language not to familiarize ourselves with their defects but rather to enrich our literature with the best they have achieved. To translate them in extracts is not to mutilate them but rather to paint them in profile and to their advantage. (trans. mine)

Gaspard de Tende is really talking about genres or text types when he points out that "it would not be advisable to translate orations that need to be treated with some leeway into a precise style, cut and dry, nor should you translate parables that need to be short and precise into a style that would allow them more leeway." Finally, the Abbé Delille is really talking about register when he writes, "I have always maintained that extreme faithfulness in translation results in extreme unfaithfulness. A word may be noble in Latin, and its French equivalent may be base."

Experts are supposed to guarantee that the trust readers place in various translations is not misplaced. But experts are not always successful, not only because they do not always reach a consensus, but also because readers tend to place less trust in the experts' stamp of approval affixed to a translation than in a translator's reputation as a good translator, or "fidus interpres," to quote Horace's famous phrase. Recent research has shown that the "fidus" (faithful) in that phrase refers much more to the personal reliability and trustworthiness of the translator than to any quality in the translation (see Norton 184).

Trust in the translator explains why bad translations continue to enjoy great popularity and sometimes even achieve a canonized status from which they can hardly be dislodged. An early example of this state of affairs can be found in Augustine's seventy-first letter, addressed to Jerome. In the letter Augustine tells the story of a bishop who introduced the use of Jerome's translation "in the church of which he [was] the pastor. He and his congregation encountered a passage from the prophet Jonah which you translated very differently from the way in which it has established itself in the mind and memory of all, and the way it has been sung for such a long time." The result was unrest, foul play was suspected, and after consultation with the local Jews, who were no help either, probably because they hugely enjoyed the dilemma of conflicting texts, the bishop "was forced to correct himself, as if he had made a mistake, since he did not want to lose all the people in his church" (letter 17).

Works Cited

Amis, Kingsley, ed. *The New Oxford Book of Light Verse.* Oxford: Oxford UP, 1987.

Augustinus, Aurelius. *The Letters of St. Augustine.* Ed. and trans. W. J. Sparrow-Simpson. London: Soc. for Promoting Christian Knowledge, 1909. N. pag.

Carlyle, Joseph D., ed. and trans. *Specimens of Arabian Poetry.* London, 1810.

Cicero, Marcus Tullius. *De oratore.* Trans. E. W. Sutton and Henry Rackham. Loeb Classical Library. Vol. 1. London: Dent; Cambridge: Harvard UP, 1947. 2 vols.

d'Alembert, Jean le Rond. *Morceaux choisis de Tacite.* Paris: Rigaud, 1784. N. pag.

Delille, Jacques. "Jacques Delille." Horguelin.

Du Bellay, Joachim. *Défense et illustration de la langue française.* Paris: Didier, 1948.

FitzGerald, Edward. *Variorum and Definitive Editions of the Poetical and Prose Writings.* Vol. 2. New York: Doubleday, 1902. 7 vols.

Goethe, Johann Wolfgang. "Goethe." Lefevere 37–41.

Gottsched, Johann Christoph. "Johann Christoph Gottsched." Lefevere 13–17.

Herder, Johann Gottfried. "Johann Gottfried Herder." Lefevere 30–34.

Horguelin, Paul, ed. *Anthologie de la manière de traduire*. Montreal: Linguatech, 1981. N. pag.

Huetius, Petrus Danielus. *De optimo genere interpretandi libri duo*. Vol. 1. The Hague: Leers, 1683. 2 vols.

Hugo, Victor. "Préface de la nouvelle traduction de Shakespeare." *Œuvres complètes de W. Shakespeare*. Trans. François-Victor Hugo. Vol. 1. Paris, 1865. i–xiv. 15 vols.

John of Trevisa. "Dialogue between a Lord and a Clerk upon Translation." *Fifteenth Century Prose and Verse*. Ed. A. W. Pollard. Westminster: Constable, 1903. N. pag.

Klopsch, Paul. "Die mittellateinische Lyrik." *Lyrik des Mittelalters*. Ed. Heinz Bergner. Vol. 1. Stuttgart: Reclam, 1983. 19–189. 2 vols.

Lefevere, André, ed. and trans. *Translating Literature: The German Tradition*. Assen: Van Gorcum, 1977.

Luther, Martin. "Martin Luther." Lefevere 7–9.

Martin, P. W. *Byron*. Cambridge: Cambridge UP, 1982.

Motte, Houdard de la. L'Iliade*: Poème, avec un discours sur Homère*. Amsterdam, 1714.

Norton, Glynn P. "Humanist Foundations of Translation Theory." *Canadian Review of Comparative Literature* 8 (1981): 178–89.

Perkins, David. *A History of Modern Poetry*. Cambridge: Harvard UP, 1976.

Polk, William R., ed. and trans. *The Golden Ode by Labid Ibn Rabiah*. Chicago: U of Chicago P, 1974.

Prévost, Antoine François. "Prévost." Horguelin.

Roscommon, William, earl of. "Essay upon Translated Verse." *English Translation Theory 1650–1800*. Ed. T. R. Steiner. Amsterdam: Van Gorcum, 1975. 75–85.

Tende, Gaspard de. *Règles de la traduction*. Paris: Damien Foucault, 1665. N. pag.

Walpole, Horace. *The Castle of Otranto. Three Gothic Novels*. Ed. Peter Fairclough. Harmondsworth, Eng.: Penguin, 1975. 27–107.

Chapter 5
Literary Translation and Beyond

It is important to teach literary translation but not just to produce translators of literature. I strongly believe that as long as the teaching of literary translation is limited to the teaching of the process, it will not be taken seriously by academic institutions at large.

The product, the finished translation, the strategies behind the making of this product, the objectives with which it is made, and, eventually, the role the product plays in a culture and a literature—all these aspects of translation will pave the way for translation studies in the institutions of academe, simply because the study of the product fits in so well with literary theory and historiography as they are practiced already. It is impossible to analyze the product without a fair knowledge of the process, but if the historical eclipse of translation studies is to be reversed, it will have to be through analyses of the product in its total cultural context, combined with the extremely topical questions of power and manipulation such an analysis is bound to raise.

I have tried to suggest a way of teaching literary translation that strikes a fair balance of the teaching of the product and the teaching of the process. I venture to think that this way of teaching literary translation could help move translation studies from the periphery of comparative literature and literary theory to a position closer to their center. In conclusion, I briefly explain why translation has been condemned to vegetate on the outskirts of literary theory and comparative literature and then suggest not only why this state of affairs should change but also how the kind of course proposed in this book could help change it.

The study of translation has been eclipsed, and the status of the production of translations lowered, in the republic of letters by a combination of at least four factors: the Romantic idea of literature as "secular scripture" and the concomitant emphasis on originality, the Romantic equation of literature with language and the concomitant equation of language with nation, the nineteenth- and early-twentieth-century philologists' insistence on reading texts in the original only, and the enormous influence exerted by New Criticism with its almost exclusive emphasis on interpretation.

Moreover, the lowering of the status of the study and production of translation unfortunately coincided with the emergence of the study of national languages and literatures in universities in many countries of Europe and in the United States. As a result, translation studies never found an appropriate niche in those universities. Departments of classics and of national languages and literatures shunned it at first, as did departments of comparative literature, for reasons to be explained a little later in this conclusion.

Translation studies' lack of an institutional base militates against the wider acceptance and more active pursuit of translation studies to the present, even in today's much more favorable intellectual climate. Too many graduate students are still gently but firmly dissuaded from going into translation studies unless they can successfully camouflage what they are doing as "reception studies." They might also find it difficult—still—to procure employment if they insist on blithely describing themselves as translation scholars. Too many scholars who translate are still not awarded appropriate recognition for their publication of translations, and they still have to organize translation courses more or less on sufferance from their departments, even though students in those departments appear to be more and more interested in those courses.

Let us now step back in history to consider the factors that contributed to the lowering of the status of translation studies.

Romantic critics, at least from the second generation of German Romanticism onward—roughly about 170 years ago—began to emphasize the originality of works of literature. That originality was valued all the more since literature came increasingly to be looked on as a kind of secular scripture on a par with Holy Scripture, and was considered ready to replace the latter as time went on. If literature was supposed to replace religion as a spiritual force, works of literature capable of performing that task could not be written by just anyone who had a way with words. Rather, they could only be written by men and women of genius and were therefore by definition unique, "original" in the fullest sense of the word.

This view of literature as secular scripture tended to cast the critic in the role of mediator between a scriptural text and its readers. It also, paradoxically, called on the critic to pronounce judgment on new candidates for possible admission to the canon of "sacral" books. It therefore effectively appointed critics to the position of guardians of the dominant poetics, the dominant idea of what literature should be.

The scholar, by contrast, would be engaged in philological work aimed at preserving and elucidating an already established canon, often in the service of the elusive ideal of objectivity. In fact, scholars would be publishing commentaries and editions, much as their predecessors had published commentaries on and editions of the Bible and the classics of antiquity, the only difference being that scholars were now free to publish commentaries on and editions of more recent and, sometimes, even contemporary texts.

It was the translators' particular misfortune at the time that they failed to reach the ideal of objectivity, an ideal largely inspired by positivistic thinking. The translator's failure to produce an objectively demonstrable "accurate" correspondence between original and translation could be exposed much more easily than the corresponding failure attendant on the philological endeavor. All it took was a simple comparison between the source text and the target text. Critics were exegetes, scholars produced useful work for the exegetes, but translators were blasphemers. When a work of literature achieves the status of scripture, any tampering with its text amounts to sacrilege. And translation was seen to be nothing if not tampering.

Romantic critics tended to identify the work of literature with the language in which it was written. They also emphasized language as the main, if not the only, constitutive factor of a nation. Just as works of literature were written by men and women of genius, nations were inspired and animated by a unique genius of their own, which expressed itself in the culture produced by each nation. Language was seen as perhaps the most obvious expression of that genius because it was both the expression and the repository of a whole culture and, therefore, of the past and present of a whole nation. If languages were unique, translation between them was extremely difficult, if not impossible. Every shift in the translation could be, and was seen as, a betrayal of the genius of a language, of a nation. Thought of in this way, translation almost amounted to high treason, and translators have, accordingly, been called traitors to their nation, usually because they were thought to weaken that nation's spirit by exposing it to foreign entities.

During most of the last century and the beginning of the present one, the philological study of literature in departments of classics and in the newly emergent departments of national languages and literatures insisted on reading in the original languages both the literature of antiquity and the literature of previous periods in the evolution of a national literature. Under these conditions the translation of literature quickly became the Achilles' heel of the young discipline of comparative literature. That young discipline could ill afford weak spots of any kind since it was still—and still is to the present, in some institutional setups—struggling to assert itself. It had to assert itself precisely against both the study of classical literatures and the study of the various national literatures that had only been recently emancipated themselves from the classical monopoly but that would keep modeling themselves on the techniques and methodology of classical philology until after the First World War.

In this intellectual climate and in this institutional context, any discipline prepared to stoop to the use of translations as anything but a useful classroom exercise, whether to check students' understanding of the actual texts read or to teach them the language of those texts, would lay itself open to attacks mounted by the philological camp against upstart comparatists. By upgrading translation and translations, comparative literature would forfeit any claim to academic, or at least institutionalized, respectability.

And yet comparative literature could not, cannot, and never will be able to do without translations if it wants to be truly comparative, that is, if it wants to be more than a Eurocentric endeavor limited to those able to speak or read a number of Indo-European languages. Comparative literature's early line of defense against philological attacks had to be ambiguous and turned out to be disastrous for translation. Many of the founders of the new discipline regarded translation the way their Victorian contemporaries regarded prostitution—as a necessary evil, to be made use of if need be, but never acknowledged. Needless to say, comparative literature has changed its attitude toward translation considerably since, but some practitioners still regard translation with a faint air of suspicion.

During the three decades in which it reigned supreme in literature departments all over the Western world, New Criticism has consistently identified meaningful study of literature with interpretation, arguing that interpretation of "scriptural" literary texts would make students into both better users of language and better human beings. As is well known, this almost exclusive emphasis on interpretation as the central endeavor of literary studies, combined with the civilizing and uplifting power ascribed to canonized texts, led to the increased reading of "Great Books" that were more and more often taken out of their historical context.

Interpretation no longer reigns supreme in literary studies. Removed from their historical context, Great Books could be regarded as timeless givens whose excellence and spiritual quality were guaranteed by generations of scholars. Once those works were put back in their historical context, it could be argued that their greatness was not wholly a natural given but, rather, a quality painstakingly constructed over the years by scholars, critics, and translators. This fact is illustrated by changes in the canon, the "imaginary library" containing all that a culture regards as its Great Books at a certain time.

Appearances to the contrary, canons are not timeless and immutable. A fairly recent addition to the Western canon is William Blake. Totally unknown in his lifetime, he now occupies a prominent niche in the canon, having been, to use the hallowed phrase, "rescued from oblivion" by editors and critics like Alexander Gilchrist, A. C. Swinburne, E. J. Ellis, and William Butler Yeats. Yet his work was probably just as much of a given; it probably possessed the same intrinsic greatness when it was unread as when it was incorporated into the reading lists of English departments and departments of comparative literature all over the world.

"Scriptural texts" are no longer seen as timelessly, universally valid. They are put back into the time in which they were written, into their social, cultural, and political context and into the network of the specific conditions of their production, distribution, and reception. This broader context allows us to analyze the various ways in which the timeless greatness of these books was actively constructed. Such an analysis reveals with amazing regularity the part played by criticism, historiography, anthologization, and translation in the construction of a Great Book. An obvious example is the construction of Omar Khayyám as a world poet in English by Edward Fitzgerald.

A view of literature that recognizes the construction of the greatness of Great Books has to recognize the part played by rewritings while not denying the intrinsic value of the books themselves. Translations, monographs, extracts in anthologies, and literary histories all have two features in common: they refer to books other than themselves and they claim to represent these books. They have no reason to exist on their own. They are not "writing" as the texts they write about are; they are "rewriting." The paradox of literary evolution appears to be that writings (the writings of William Blake, for example) hardly ever make it on their own. Rather, rewritings (Gilchrist, Swinburne, Ellis, Yeats, anthologizers and literary historians, countless translators of Blake) seem to be a vital factor in determining whether a writing does or does not secure the label of greatness.

Writings that are not rewritten in one way or another tend to sink without a trace. The feminist classics of the twenties, thirties, and forties, for example, now actively republished by feminist and other presses, presumably have the same essential qualities now as when they were first published. They were reclaimed from oblivion only when feminist criticism had helped establish a more receptive climate for them.

A view of literature that sees greatness as partly constructed will no longer be dominated by the production of interpretations of what is given. The critic will no longer be the mediator, the priestlike figure. The canon will no longer be accepted as self-evident or interpreted in its timeless given perfection. Instead, the critic will be the historian, the sociologist, the technician, and the canon will be challenged, changed, and analyzed in its historical evolution.

In such a view of literature the translator can become a technician among others, making texts available for study. The translation scholar can analyze the part played by translations in the constitution and revision of various canons and in the struggle between various poetics. The translation scholar can analyze the reception of foreign works inside a national literature. If translation scholars proceed to study other rewritings of literature as well, they can also analyze most of the parts of the mechanism that confers greatness on certain works of literature at certain times. They can take that mechanism apart in its ideological and poetological components and trace its workings through the intermediary of the educational system and the media.

Other factors that have historically contributed to a certain reluctance either to use or to study translations have in their turn been weakened by history. The enormous influx of students with different intellectual backgrounds into universities since the end of the Second World War has made the insistence on reading works of literature in the original language impossible to maintain. If syllabi are expanded in the near future to include works of literature written in Asian and African languages, the use of translations will increase even more. As it is, courses in world literature or simply literature, as taught in American universities at the moment, quietly undermine the identification of a work of literature with the language in which it is written by teaching more or less all literature in English. Comparative literature with its emphasis on influence and the reconstruction of the genealogy of works of literature beyond the boundaries of national literatures has, in its turn, increasingly questioned the Romantic tenet of originality.

It is to be hoped that the weakening of the disinclination for translation studies will also spell the end of the discrimination against translation as a scholarly activity and against young scholars who have chosen to demonstrate their competence (receive their doctorate) in any way that involves translation. Institutional inertia is largely responsible for the ability of a dissertation to command more academic prestige than a "mere" translation can. But it should not be hard to see that a translation into language B of a work considered valuable in culture A might be of more interest, let alone importance, than a dissertation written in language B on the use of, say, similes in the work written in language A. It should also be remembered that scholars who translate make the works they translate potentially much more influential outside academe. At the same time, their translations are grounded in knowledge about the source and target texts and the source and target languages and cultures that does not come easily to most of the gifted amateurs routinely entrusted with the task of translating.

If scholars translate, if they analyze translations, and if they analyze the part played by translations in the receiving literatures and cultures, chances are not only that we shall learn much more about the workings of the complex phenomenon known as culture, but also that translation studies may come to occupy a place in academe that reflects the importance of translation in the culture that has produced academe. This book tries to prepare prospective scholars for the three tasks listed.

Chapter 6

Topics for Classroom Teaching and Research

Much work remains to be done in the study of translation. New translations need to be made, existing translations need to be analyzed, and the role played by translations in the development of literatures and cultures needs to be further elucidated. None of this can be done exhaustively or even conclusively within the institutional framework of the translation course. Instructors should make students aware of the possibilities for translating and research and encourage them to undertake larger projects for their MA and doctoral dissertations.

This section contains a list of possible topics for further research. Students can devote term papers or presentations to an aspect or a survey of one of these topics. They should be encouraged to build case studies around translations into or out of their native literatures to try to shed more light on the issues covered, to refine and answer the questions and, perhaps best of all, to supplement them with further questions.

The Role of the Audience

Which audience do translators target as the potential and likely recipient of their translations? Why? What do either translators or the target group (or both) hope to achieve by the translation? To what extent does this intention influence the actual production of particular translations? To what extent does it influence the selection of particular texts for translating? What happens when there is a change in a particular target group's ideology? in its poetics? in both? Does the composition of an audience make it impossible, or at least impractical, to translate certain texts? In which historical periods? What happens if an audience does not want to abandon a bad translation?

The Role of the Patron

Who commissions translations, and why? Who publishes them, and why? Do publishers publish translations purely for profit, or are there publishers (most publishing houses owned by organizations) whose translation list betrays an interest in cultural politics? What are the cultural politics of major publishing houses regarding translation, and why are they pursued? How do proponents of alternative poetics get their translations published after all? Do they always or usually have to publish themselves? What part do anthologies play in this respect? How does book publication differ from publication in journals? What about the comparative prestige of various imprints? What about the identification of an imprint with a poetics? To what extent do established publishers integrate the proponents of alternative poetics into the mainstream? To what extent does a publisher actively try to influence the development of a literature by the publication of translations? What does this activity imply for the selection and production of translations? To what extent do the policies of trade publishers and scholarly publishers differ with regard to publishing translations? Why are the policies different?

Ethnocentricity and Eurocentricity

What, if anything, do translators feel they have to screen out and what leave in when translating from a European to a non-European language, and vice versa? Is material excluded or included for ideological or poetological reasons? Or both? Do translators try to use European works to influence the development of non-European literatures, and vice versa? What is the attitude of the translators toward their source and target culture readers? Do non-European translators who regard European culture as superior to their own translate differently from non-European translators who do not do so? Are there Eurocentric translations, that is, translations that ruthlessly adapt non-European ideologies and universes of discourse to a European model? What part did such translations play in colonization or other attempts to establish European domination?

Central Texts

Which texts does a culture consider central to its identity as a culture? Do they include only ideological texts (the King James Version of the Bible, for instance), or literary texts (Shakespeare) as well? If the central texts embody the identity of a culture, what measures does that culture try to take to ensure that those texts survive and flourish? What implications do these activities have for potential translators? Are translators encouraged or discouraged?

What if—as in Europe for roughly fifteen centuries—the central text of a culture is itself a translation? What measures are taken to ensure that translations "faithfully" represent the source text? Can those measures ever be effective? To what extent? How do various groups of different ideological persuasions translate the same central text? For what purpose?

What about the survival of translations of central texts when the translations no longer function as such (the Luther Bible)? What part do they continue to play in their culture?

Usurpation of Authority

Who uses translation to introduce certain concepts into a given culture or certain devices into a given literature? Why? Who tries to resist the introduction of either or both? When and where does the phenomenon of pseudotranslation appear, and what is its use in cultural and literary politics? Why do authors of pseudotranslations not speak in their own names? Why do translators occupy a relatively ambiguous position (half in, half out) in a culture? What implications does that position have for cultural politics? What happens when a text introduced into one culture as a pseudotranslation (*Ossian*) is translated in its turn (by Goethe) and is done so with great success? How can one explain the discrepancy when a work is far more successful in translation than in its original language (as was, for instance, Pierre Le Tourneur's French translation of Edward Young's *Night Thoughts*, which enjoyed a lukewarm reception in England but was enormously popular in France)?

Translation Bestowing Authority

What strategies do emerging languages use to prove their worth by translation? What did European languages do during the Renaissance, and what are African languages doing now? What effect does translation have on the vocabulary of a language? Do translators adopt different strategies when they are translating into or out of a language of authority? Why and in what circumstances is a language of authority used to introduce to a wider audience writers who do not really write in it? Why are some works of literature available in translations in a language of authority and others not? What implications does this have for the inclusion of some literary works in the canon of world literature? Can you produce examples of forgotten or "untranslatable" great authors who have never been able to move beyond the confines of their own language? Why have they not been translated?

Resistance to Translation

Why do cultures and literatures resist translation? Is there something in their self-estimation, ideology, political and/or social organization that predisposes them to adopt this attitude?

In which circumstances are translators faced with the problems of acculturation? What strategies do they use to transfer universe-of-discourse features from one culture into another? What arguments can be marshaled in favor of and against naturalizing the "exotic" or making it even more so? To what extent does the central or less central status of the source or target culture influence these strategies? To what extent are these strategies analogous to those developed by African and other Third World writers writing in a language of authority that is not their native tongue?

What good or ill fortune befalls the source text if translators understand or fail to understand its universe of discourse? What can be done to correct the wrong image of a culture projected by previous translations (FitzGerald's *Omar Khayyám*) that have acquired a near-canonized status in the target culture?

Poetics

How can translation be used as a device to measure the strength and weakness of a poetics in a culture at a certain time? How can it be used to reveal the degree to which a certain poetics has been interiorized? How is translation used as a weapon in the struggle between different poetics? What criteria are used for the selection of texts to be translated and for the production of translations as weapons in this respect? How are these translations distributed through publication in books and journals?

Which problems arise when the transplantation of genres from one literature or culture to another is attempted? Is it possible to solve any or all of them? How? Is "untranslatability" the result of the lack of a convincing analog on the level of poetics in the target literature? Are there other reasons for untranslatability? Does untranslatability mean the same thing as the decision not to translate? What repercussions does untranslatability have on the inclusion of certain works, authors, literatures in the canon of world literature?

Trust, Expertise, and History

How are rules for translating formulated at different moments in history? Are these rules effective? Are they even followed? To what extent? What do the rules reveal about a culture's self-image? How do rules for translating change? Under what kind of pressure?

Why do bad translations survive? What is their position in the target culture? What implications does their continued existence have for the assessment of quality in translation and for the effective application of rules?

Image

Who constructs what image of a writer, a work, a literature, a culture, and why? How are those images constructed? What elements of the reality of the original are skewed to construct the desired image, and in what way? How long does the image so constructed survive in the target literature or culture? What are the consequences of the survival of such an image? How can translation be used for propaganda?

There is, once again, much work to be done in the study of literary translation by literary scholars whose attitude allows them to undertake it. But the work is somewhat less glamorous than what is currently performed in criticism and theory. It does not confer the status of cultural guru, and it does not reward sweeping generalizations—perhaps the major inconvenience connected with it. It is likely to teach us more about the development and interaction of literatures and cultures. This potential puts the study of literary translation and other forms of rewriting near the center of the new dispensation of literary studies that has begun to take shape in a time that increasingly doubts that anything—including the collection of images of ourselves and others, of animals, objects, and locations we call "reality" for short—is given and therefore guaranteed and that increasingly stresses the manipulated "construction" of much of what has been taken for granted.

Suggestions for Further Reading

Bibliographies always reflect their compiler's judgment; this one also reflects his limitations. It contains most of the important contributions to the field of literary translation and cross-cultural communication published in Europe and the Americas during the last three decades, with some exceptions made for older seminal contributions. It does not contain language-pair-specific contributions, except when they go beyond simple comparisons of languages or texts and deal with the influence exerted by translations on the evolution of literatures. In the interest of accessibility, contributions originally written in less widely spoken languages, such as Bulgarian, Czech, Dutch, and Slovak, have been listed in their English, French, or German translations. Regrettably, the list omits those contributions to the theory of translation that are written in Central European, Russian, and non-Western languages and have not been translated into a "major" Western language.

Adams, R. *Proteus, His Lies, His Truth: Discussions on Literary Translation.* New York: Norton, 1973.

Alsina, José. "Teoría de la traducción." *Literatura Griega.* Ed. José Alsina. Barcelona: Ariel, 1983. 425–44.

Amos, Flora Ross. *Early Theories of Translation.* New York: Octagon, 1973.

Apel, Friedmar. *Literarische Übersetzung.* Stuttgart: Metzler, 1982.

——— . *Sprachbewegung: Eine historisch-poetologische Untersuchung zum Problem des Übersetzens.* Heidelberg: Carl Winter, 1982.

Apter, Ronnie. *Digging for the Treasure: Translation after Pound.* New York: Lang, 1984.

Argente, Joan. "Significació literal, significació social i traducció." *Cuadernos de traducción e interpretación* 3 (1983): 135–42.

Arntz, Reiner, and Gisela Thomé, eds. *Übersetzungswissenschaft: Ergebnisse und Perspektiven. Festschrift für Wolfram Wilss zum fünfundsechzigsten Geburtstag.* Tübingen: Narr, 1990.

Arrowsmith, William, and Roger Shattuck, eds. *The Craft and Context of Translation.* Austin: U of Texas P, 1961.

Assises de la traduction littéraire 4. Arles: Actes Sud, 1988.

Assises de la traduction littéraire 5. Arles: Actes Sud, 1989.

Ayala, Francisco. *Problemas de la traducción.* Madrid: Taurus, 1965.

Balcerzan, Edward. "La traduction, art d'interpréter." Holmes, *Nature* 3–22.
Ballard, Michel. *La traduction: De la théorie à la didactique.* Lille: U de Lille, 1984.
Ballard, Michel, et al. *La traduction plurielle.* Lille: U de Lille, 1990.
Barchudarow, Lev. *Sprache und Übersetzung.* Leipzig: Enzyklopädie, 1979.
———. "Übersetzungstheorie als vergleichende Textlinguistik." *Übersetzungs-wissenschaftliche Beiträge* 1 (1977): 7–13.
Barnwell, Katherine. "Testing the Translation." *Bible Translator* 28.4 (1977): 425–32.
———. "Towards Acceptable Translations." *Notes on Translation* 95 (1983): 19–25.
Barrass, Tine. "The Function of Translated Literature within a National Literature: The Example of Sixteenth-Century Spain." Holmes, Lambert, and Broeck 181–203.
Bassnett, Susan. "Translating Spatial Poetry: An Examination of Theatre Texts in Performance." Holmes, Lambert and Broeck 161–76.
———. *Translation Studies.* London: Methuen, 1980.
Bassnett, Susan, and André Lefevere, eds. *Translation, History and Culture.* London: Pinter, 1990.
Bausch, Karl-Richard, Josef Klegraf, and Wolfram Wilss, eds. *The Science of Translation: An Analytical Bibliography.* Tübingen: Spangenberg, 1971. 2 vols.
Beaugrande, Robert Alain de. *Factors in a Theory of Poetic Translating.* Assen: Van Gorcum, 1978.
———. "Towards a Semiotic Theory of Literary Translating." Wilss, *Semiotik* 23–42.
Beekman, John. "Anthropology and the Translation of New Testament Key Terms." *Notes on Translation* 80 (1980): 32–42.
Beer, Jeanette, ed. *Medieval Translators and Their Craft.* Kalamazoo: Western Michigan U, 1989.
Benjamin, Andrew. *Translation and the Nature of Philosophy.* London: Routledge, 1989.
Benjamin, Walter. "Die Aufgabe des Übersetzers." *Schriften.* Vol. 1. Frankfurt: Suhrkamp, 1955. 40–45.
Berman, Antoine. *L'épreuve de l'étranger.* Paris: Gallimard, 1984.
———. "La traduction comme épreuve de l'étranger." *Texte* 4 (1986): 67–81.
———. "La traduction et la lettre." *Les Tours de Babel.* [Maurezin?]: Trans-Europ-Repress, 1985. 35–150.
Biguenet, John, and Rainer Schulte, eds. *The Craft of Translation.* Chicago: U of Chicago P, 1989.
Brislin, Richard W., ed. *Translation: Applications and Research.* New York: Gardner, 1976.
Brislin, Richard W., Walter J. Lonner, and Robert M. Thorndike. *Cross-Cultural Research Methods.* New York: Wiley, 1973.
Brisset, Annie. "La traduction comme transformation paradoxale." *Texte* 4 (1986): 191–207.

Broeck, Raymond van den. "Generic Shifts in Translated Literary Texts." Hermans, *Literary* 104–16.

———. "The Limits the Translatability Exemplified by Metaphor Translation." Even-Zohar and Toury 73–87.

———. "Toward a Text-Type-Oriented Theory of Translation." Poulsen 82–96.

———. "Translating for the Theatre." *Linguistica Antverpiensia* 20 (1986): 96–110.

Brotherton, Alex. "Anomalies in Source Texts as a Translation Factor." *Van taal tot taal* 30 (1986): 99–107.

Brower, Reuben A. *Mirror on Mirror: Translation, Imitation, Parody.* Cambridge: Harvard UP, 1974.

———, ed. *On Translation.* Cambridge: Harvard UP, 1959.

Bruns, Alken. *Übersetzung als Rezeption.* Neumünster: Wachholtz, 1977.

Bühler, Hildegund. "Language and Translation: Translating and Interpreting as a Profession." *Annual Review of Applied Linguistics* 7 (1986): 105–19.

———. "Suprasentential Semantics and Translation." *Meta* 24 (1979): 451–57.

Campos, Haroldo de. "De la traducción como creación y como crítica." *Quimera* 9 (1981): 30–37.

Cantera Ortiz de Urbina, Jesús. "Civilización y traducción." *Filología Moderna* 63-64 (1978): 167–95.

Caproni, Giorgio. "Divagazioni sul tradurre." *Premio 21–29.*

Cary, Edmond. *Comment faut-il tradiure?* Lille: PU de Lille, 1985.

Cary, Edmond, and Rudolph Jumpelt, eds. *Quality in Translation.* New York: Macmillan, 1963.

Casares, Angel. *Dos palabres sobre las palabras: Apuntes sobre la traducción y sus problemas.* Río Piedras: U of Puerto Rico P, 1982.

Castro Viejo, Antonio, Encarnación Garcia Fernandez, and Carmen Ramos Sarasa, eds. *La traducción: Arte y técnica.* Madrid: Ministerio de Educación y Ciencias, 1984.

Catford, John C. *A Linguistic Theory of Translation.* London: Oxford UP, 1965.

Cigada, Sergio. "La traduzione come strumento di analisi critica del testo letterario." *Processo traduttivi: Teorie ed applicazioni.* Brescia: La Scuola, 1982. 187–99.

Cohen, John M. *English Translators and Translations.* London: Longmans, 1962.

Colloque sur la traduction poétique. Paris: Gallimard, 1978.

Coseriu, Eugenio. "Falsche und richtige Fragestellungen in der Übersetzungstheorie." Grähs, Korlén, and Malmberg 17–32.

Dagut, Menachim. "Can 'Metaphor' Be Translated?" *Babel* 22 (1976): 21–33.

———. " 'Semantic Voids' as a Problem in the Translation Process." Even-Zohar and Toury 61–71.

Davie, Donald. *Poetry in Translation.* Milton Keynes, Eng.: Open UP, 1975.

Day Lewis, Cecil. *On Translating Poetry.* Abingdon-on-Thames: Abbey, 1970.

Della Volpe, Galvano. *Critica del gusto.* Milan: Feltrinelli, 1972.

De Luca, Iginio. "Noterella sulla traduzione letteraria e poetica." *Premio* 52–59.

Derrida, Jacques. "Des Tours de Babel." Graham 165–208.

D'hulst, Lieven. "The Conflict of Translational Models in France (End of 18th–Beginning of 19th Century)." *Dispositio* 7 (1982): 41–52.

———. "Les variantes textuelles des traductions littéraires." Even-Zohar and Toury 133–41.

Diaz-Diocaretz, Myriam. *Translating in Poetic Discourse*. Amsterdam: Benjamins, 1985.

Doron, Marcia Nita, and Marilyn Gaddis Rose. "The Economics and Politics of Translation." Rose, *Translation Spectrum* 160–67.

Douma, Felix J. "On Reviewing a Translation." *Meta* 17 (1972): 87–101.

Drescher, Horst W., and Signe Scheffzek, eds. *Theorie und Praxis des Übersetzens und Dolmetschens*. Bern: Lang, 1976.

Dressler, Wolfgang. "Der Beitrag der Textlinguistik zur Übersetzungs-wissenschaft." Kapp, *Übersetzer* 61–71.

———. "Textgrammatische Invarianz in Übersetzungen?" *Textsorten*. Ed. Elizabeth Gülich and Wolfgang Raible. Frankfurt: Athenäum, 1972. 98–106.

Ellis, Roger, et al., eds. *The Medieval Translator: The Theory and Practice of Translation in the Middle Ages*. Cambridge, Eng.: Brewer, 1989.

Elvira-Hernandez, Juan. *Traiciones del traductor*. Piedrahita, Sp.: Sexifirmo, 1978.

Enkvist, Nils Erik. "Contrastive Text Linguistics and Translation." Grähs, Korlén, and Malmberg. 169–88.

Escarpit, René. " 'Creative Treason' as a Key to Literature." *Yearbook of Comparative and General Literature* 10 (1961): 16–21.

Etkind, Efim. *Essay de poétique de la traduction poétique*. Lausanne: Age d'homme, 1982.

———. "La stylistique comparée, base de l'art de traduire." *Babel* 13 (1967): 22–30.

———. "La traduction et les courants littéraires." Holmes, Lambert, and Broeck 128–41.

Even-Zohar, Itamar. *Papers in Historical Poetics*. Tel Aviv: Porter Inst. for Poetics and Semiotics, 1978.

———. "Translation Theory Today: A Call for Transfer Theory." Even-Zohar and Toury 1–7.

Even-Zohar, Itamar, and Gideon Toury, eds. *Translation Theory and Intercultural Relations*. Spec. issue of *Poetics Today* 2.4 (1981): v–xi, 1–239.

Fabian, Johannes. *Language and Colonial Power: The Appropriation of Swahili in the Former Belgian Congo 1880–1938*. New York: Cambridge UP, 1986.

Fawcett, Peter. "Teaching Translation Theory." *Meta* 26 (1981): 141–47.

Fedorov, Andrej. *Introduction à la théorie de la traduction*. Brussels: Ecole Supérieure de Traducteurs et d'Interprètes, 1968.

———. "The Problem of Verse Translation." *Linguistics* 137 (1974): 13–29.

Finlay, Ian F. *Translating*. London: Teach Yourself, 1971.

Firth, John Rupert. *The Tongues of Men and Speech*. London: Oxford UP, 1968.

Flamand, Jacques. *Ecrire et traduire*. Ottawa: Vermillon, 1983.

Frank, Armin Paul. "Theories and Theory of Literary Translation." *Literary Theory and Criticism*. Ed. Joseph P. Strelka. Vol. 1. Bern: Lang, 1984. 203–21.

———. "Towards a Cultural History of Literary Translation." *REAL* 4 (1986): 317–80.

Frawley, William, ed. *Translation: Literary, Linguistic, and Philosophical Perspectives*. Newark: U of Delaware P, 1984.

Friedrich, Hugo. *Zur Frage der Übersetzungskunst*. Heidelberg: Winter, 1965.

Gara, Ladislas, et al., eds. *Translation and Translators*. London: Intl. PEN, 1963.

Garcia Yebra, Valentin. "Las dos fases de la traducción de textos clásicos latinos y griegos." *Cuadernos de traducción e interpretación* 7 (1986): 7–17.

———. *En torno a la traducción*. Madrid: Gredos, 1983.

———. *Teoría y práctica de la traducción*. Madrid: Gredos, 1982.

Gorp, Hendrik van. "La traduction littéraire parmi les autres métatextes." Holmes, Lambert, and Broeck 101–16.

———. "Traductions et évolution d'un genre littéraire." Even-Zohar and Toury 209–19.

Graham, Joseph F., ed. *Difference in Translation*. Ithaca: Cornell UP, 1985.

Grähs, Lillebill, Gustav Korlén, and Bertil Malmberg, eds. *Theory and Practice of Translation*. Nobel Symposium 39. Bern: Lang, 1978.

Gruber, Edith Maria. "The Significance of Translation for the Development of Spanish Romanticism." Hermans, *Literary* 57–66.

Guenthner, Franz, and M. Guenthner-Reutter, eds. *Meaning and Translation: Philosophical and Linguistic Approaches*. New York: New York UP, 1978.

Guillerm, Luce. "L'auteur, les modèles et le pouvoir; ou, Le topique de la traduction au seizième siècle en France." *Revue des sciences humaines* 52 (1980): 5–31.

———. "L'intertextualité démontée: Le discours sur la traduction." *Littérature* 55 (1984): 54–63.

Güttinger, Fritz. *Zielsprache*. Zurich: Manesse, 1963.

Haas, Willy. "The Theory of Translation." *Philosophy* 37 (1962): 208–28.

Hartmann, Reinhard. "Contrastive Textology and Translation." *Kontrastive Linguistik und Übersetzungswissenschaft*. Ed. Wolfgang Kühlwein, Gisela Thomé, and Wolfram Wilss. Munich: Fink, 1981. 200–08.

Hébert, Anne, and Frank Scott. *Dialogue sur la traduction*. Montreal: HMH, 1970.

Hermans, Theo, ed. "Literary Translation: The Birth of a Concept." Hermans, *Literary* 28–42.

———. *Literary Translation and Literary System*. Spec. issue of *New Comparison* 1.1 (1986): 5–125.

———, ed. *The Manipulation of Literature: Studies in Literary Translation*. London: Croom Helm, 1985.

Hoffmann, Norbert. *Redundanz und Äquivalenz in der literarischen Übersetzung*. Tübingen: Niemeyer, 1980.

Holmes, James S. "A Basic Bibliography of Books on Translation Studies 1956–1976." Holmes, Lambert, and Broeck 236–60.

———. "The Cross-Temporal Factor in Verse Translation." *Slavica Slovaca* 6 (1971): 326–34.

———. "Describing Literary Translations: Models and Methods." Holmes, Lambert, and Broeck 69–82.

———. "Forms of Verse Translation and the Translation of Verse Form." *Babel* 15 (1969): 195–201.

———, ed. *The Nature of Translation*. The Hague: Mouton; Bratislava: Slovak Acad. of Sciences, 1970.

———. "The State of Two Arts: Literary Translation and Translation Studies in the West Today." *Der Übersetzer und seine Stellung in der Öffentlichkeit.* Ed. Hildegund Bühler. Vienna: FIT, 1985. 147–53.

———. *Translated!* Ed. Raymond van den Broeck. Amsterdam: Rodopi, 1988.

Holmes, James S., José Lambert, and Raymond van den Broeck, eds. *Literature and Translation: New Perspectives in Literary Studies*. Louvain: Acco, 1978.

Holst-Mänttäri, Justa. *Translatorisches Handeln*. Helsinki: Suomalainen Tiedeakatemia, 1984.

Homel, David, and Sherry Simon, eds. *Mapping Literature*. Montreal: Véhicule, 1988.

Hönig, Hans G., and Paul Kussmaul. *Strategie der Übersetzung*. Tübingen: Narr, 1982.

Hoof, Henri van. *Internationale Bibliographie der Übersetzung/International Bibliography of Translation*. Pullach: Dokumentation, 1973.

———. *Petite histoire de la traduction, en Occident*. Louvain la Neuve: Peeters, 1986.

Horguelin, Paul A., ed. *La traduction, une profession/Translating, a Profession*. Montreal: Conseil des Traducteurs et Interprètes du Canada, 1978.

House, Juliane. *A Model for Translation Quality Assessment*. Tübingen: Narr, 1977.

House, Juliane, and Shoshana Blum-kulka, eds. *Interlingual and Intercultural Communication*. Tübingen: Narr, 1986.

Italiaander, Rolf, ed. *Übersetzen*. Frankfurt: Athenäum, 1965.

Ivanov, V. V. "La traduction poétique à la lumière de la linguistique." *Change* 14 (1973): 45–60.

Ivir, Vladimir. "Linguistic and Extra-linguistic Considerations in Translation." *Studia Romanica et Anglica Zagrebiensia* 33-36 (1972–73): 615–26.

———. "Social Aspects of Translation." *Studia Romanica et Anglica Zagrebiensia* 39 (1975): 205–13.

Izzo, Carlo. "Responsibilità del traduttore." *Friendship's Garland: Essays Presented to Mario Praz on his Seventieth Birthday.* Ed. Vittorio Gabrieli. Vol. 2. Rome: Storia e Letteratura, 1966. 361–80.

Jäger, Gert. *Translation und Translationslinguistik*. Halle: Niemeyer, 1975.

———. "Zu Gegenstand und Zielen der Übersetzungswissenschaft." *Übersetzungswissenschaftliche Beiträge* 1 (1977): 14–26.

Jäger, Gert, and Albrecht Neubert, eds. *Bedeutung und Translation*. Leipzig: Enzyklopädie, 1986.

Jakobson, Roman. "On Linguistic Aspects of Translation." Brower, *On Translation* 232–39.

Kachroo, Balkrishan. "Textual Cohesion and Translation." *Meta* 29 (1984): 128–34.

Kade, Otto. *Die Sprachmittlung als gesellschaftliche Erscheinung und Gegenstand wissenschaftlicher Untersuchung.* Leipzig: Enzyklopädie, 1979.

————. "Zu einigen Grundlagen der allgemeinen Übersetzungstheorie." *Fremdsprachen* 3 (1965): 163–77.

————. "Zu einigen Grundpositionen bei der theoretischen Erklärung der Sprachmittlung als menschlicher Tätigkeit." *Übersetzungswissenschaftliche Beiträge* 1 (1977): 27–43.

————. *Zufall und Gesetzmässigkeit in der Übersetzung.* Leipzig: Enzyklopädie, 1968.

————. "Zum Verhältnis von Translation und Transformation." Beiheft of *Fremdsprachen* 3-4 (1971): 7–26.

————. "Zum Zusammenhang zwischen Weltanschauung und Methoden in der Übersetzungstheorie." *Zeitschrift für Phonetik, Sprachwissenschaft und Kommunikationsforschung* 31(1978): 506–11.

————. "Zur Anwendung verschiedener Realisationsformen der Translation." *Linguistische Arbeitsberichte* 7 (1973): 75–119.

Kaemmerling, Ekkehard. "Dramenübersetzung und semiotische Übersetzungsanalyse." *Literatursemiotik 2.* Ed. Achim Eschbach and Wendelin Rader. Tübingen: Narr, 1980. 55–85.

Kapp, Volker. "Die literarische Übersetzung zwischen Landeskunde und Übersetzungskritik." Kapp, *Übersetzer* 134–46.

————, ed. *Übersetzer und Dolmetscher.* Heidelberg: Quelle, 1974.

————. "Übersetzungswissenschaft und vergleichende Stilistik." Drescher and Scheffzek 33–47.

Katny, Andrzej, ed. *Studien zur kontrastiven Linguistik und literarischen Übersetzung.* Frankfurt: Lang, 1989.

Kelly, Louis G. *The True Interpreter: A History of Translation Theory and Practice in the West.* Oxford: Blackwell, 1979.

Kittel, Harald, ed. *Die literarische Übersetzung: Stand und Perspektiven ihrer Erforschung.* Berlin: Schmidt, 1988.

Kloepfer, Rolf. "Intra- and Intercultural Translation." Even-Zohar and Toury 29–37.

————. *Die Theorie der literarischen Übersetzung.* Munich: Fink, 1975.

Klor de Alva, Jorge. "Language, Politics and Translation: Colonial Discourse and Classical Nahuatl in New Spain." Warren 143–62.

Koch, Hans-Albrecht, ed. *Sprachkunst und Übersetzung.* Bern: Lang, 1983.

Koller, Werner. *Einführung in die Übersetzungswissenschaft.* Heidelberg: Quelle, 1979.

————. *Grundprobleme der Übersetzungstheorie.* Bern: Francke, 1972.

————. "Zur Geschichtlichkeit von Übersetzungstheorie, Sprachpraxis und Übersetzungsdidaktik." Wilss and Thomé 37–45.

Korpel, Luc. "The Discourse on Translation in the Netherlands (1750–1800)." Hermans, *Literary* 43–56.

Ladmiral, Jean-René, ed. *La traduction.* Paris: Didier, 1972.

———. *Traduire: Théorèmes pour la traduction.* Paris: Payot, 1979.

Lambert, José. "Echanges littéraires et traduction." Holmes, Lambert, and Broeck 142–60.

———. "Production, tradition, et importation: Une clef pour la description de la littérature et de la littérature en traduction." *Revue canadienne de littérature comparée* 7 (1980): 246–52.

———. "Théorie de la littérature et théorie de la traduction en France." Even-Zohar and Toury 161–70.

———. "La traduction en France à l'époque romantique." *Revue de littérature comparée* 49 (1975): 396–412.

———. "Traduction et technique romanesque." *Quattordicèsimo congresso internationale de linguistica e filologia romanza.* Ed. A. Varvaro. Vol. 2. Naples: Macchiaroli; Amsterdam: Benjamins, 1977. 653–68.

Lambert, José, and André Lefevere. "Traduction, traduction littéraire et littérature comparée." Horguelin 329–42.

Larson, Mildred. *Meaning-Based Translation.* Lanham: UP of America, 1984.

Lawendowski, Boguslaw. "On Semiotic Aspects of Translation." *Sight, Sound, and Sense.* Ed. Thomas A. Sebeok. Bloomington: Indiana UP, 1978. 264–82.

Lefevere, André, and Kenneth David Jackson, eds. *The Art and Science of Translation.* Spec. issue of *Dispositio* 7.19-20-21 (1982): 4–247.

———. " 'Beyond Interpretation' or the Business of Rewriting." *Comparative Literature Studies* 24 (1987): 17–39.

———. "Systems Thinking and Cultural Relativism." *Jadavpur Journal of Comparative Literature* 26-27 (1988–89): 55–68.

———. "That Structure in the Dialect of Men Interpreted." Shaffer 87–100.

———. *Translating Poetry: Seven Strategies and a Blueprint.* Amsterdam: Van Gorcum, 1975.

———. "Translation and/in Comparative Literature." *Yearbook of Comparative and General Literature* 35 (1986): 40–50.

———. "Translation: Its Genealogy in the West." Bassnett and Lefevere 14–28.

———. "Why Waste Our Time on Rewrites? The Trouble with Interpretation and the Role of Rewriting in an Alternative Paradigm." Hermans, *Manipulation* 215–43.

Lefevere, André, and Susan Bassnett. "Proust's Grandmother and the Thousand and One Nights." Bassnett and Lefevere 1–13.

Levy, Jiří. *Die literarische Übersetzung.* Frankfurt: Athenäum, 1969.

———. "Translation as a Decision Process." *To Honor Roman Jakobson.* The Hague: Mouton, 1967. 1171–82.

———. "The Translation of Verbal Art." *Semiotics of Art.* Ed. Ladislav Matejka and Irvin R. Titunik. Cambridge: MIT P, 1976. 218–64.

———. "Will Translation Theory Be of Use to Translators?" Italiaander 77–82.

Lingenfelter, Sherwood G. "Social Anthropology and Translation." *Notes on Translation* 116 (1986): 30–46.

Loewen, Jacob A. "Culture, Meaning and Translation." *The Bible Translator* 15 (1964): 189–94.

Longacre, Robert. *Translation: A Cable of Many Strands.* Honolulu: U of Hawaii P, 1973.

Lopez Morales, Humberto. *Estructura interna, estructura externa y traducción.* Río Piedras: Publicaciones de la Faculdad de Humanidades, 1974.

Ludskanov, Alexander. "A propos des problèmes théoriques de la traduction." *T. A. Informations* 1 (1968): 107–12.

———. "A Semiotic Approach to the Theory of Translation." *Language Sciences* 35 (Apr. 1975): 5–8.

———. *Traduction humaine et traduction mécanique.* Paris: Dunoc, 1969.

Macura, Vladimir. "Culture as Translation." Bassnett and Lefevere 64–70.

Magaña Anthauer, Juanita. "Algunas consideraciones acerca de los problemas de traducción." *Estudios filológicos* 1 (1965): 153–63.

Magnuson, Gunnar, and Steffan Wahlen, eds. *Teaching Translation.* Stockholm: Stockholm UP, 1988.

Maison, Elvira. *Estudios sobre la traducción.* Madrid: Literatura Americana Reunida, 1983.

Malblanc, Alfred. *Stylistique comparée du français et de l'allemand: Essai de représentation comparée et étude de traduction.* Paris: Didier, 1963.

Marias Franco, Javier. "La traducción de poesía: Ausencia y memoria." *Primer Simposio* 163–73.

Maurer, Karl. "Die literarische Übersetzung als Form fremdbestimmter Textkonstitution." *Poetica* 8 (1976): 233–57.

McDonald, Christie, ed. *The Ear of the Other: Autobiography, Transference, Translation.* Lincoln: U of Nebraska P, 1988.

McFarlane, James. "Modes of Translation." *Durham University Journal* 19 (1953): 77–93.

Merino, Waldo. "Problemes y dificultades de la traducción." Castro Viejo, Garcia Fernandez, and Ramos Sarasa 61–71.

———. "Traduttore traditore: Riesgos y peligros de la traducción." *Estudios humanísticos* 5 (1983): 39–54.

Meschonnic, Henri. *Pour la poétique 2.* Paris: Gallimard, 1973.

Meyer, Martin, ed. *Vom Übersetzen.* Munich: Hanser, 1990.

Mounin, Georges. *Les belles infidèles.* Paris: Cahiers du Sud, 1955.

———. "La notion de qualité en matière de traduction littéraire." Cary and Jumpelt 50–57.

———. *Les problèmes théoriques de la traduction.* Paris: Gallimard, 1963.

Neira, Jesús. "La traducción: Possibilidades y límites." *Archivum* 21 (1971): 337–57.

———. *Die Übersetzung: Geschichte, Theorie, Anwendung.* Munich: Nymphenburger, 1967.

Neubert, Albrecht, ed. *Grundfragen der Übersetzungswissenschaft.* Beiheft 2 of *Fremdsprachen.* Leipzig: Enzyklopädie, 1968.

———. "Pragmatische Aspekte der Übersetzung." Neubert, *Grundfragen* 21–33.

———. "Semantik der Übersetzungswissenschaft." *Probleme der strukturellen Grammatik und Semantik.* Ed. R. Ruzicka. Halle: Niemeyer, 1968. 199–208.

———. "Text-Bound Translation Teaching." Wilss and Thomé 61–70.

———. "Theorie und Praxis für die Übersetzungswissenschaft." *Linguistische Arbeitsberichte* 7 (1973): 120–44.

———. "Translation, Interpretation and Text Linguistics." *Studia linguistica* 1 (1981): 130–45.

———. "Übersetzungswissenschaft in soziolinguistischer Sicht." *Übersetzungswissenschaftliche Beiträge* 1 (1977): 52–59.

Neubert, Albrecht, and Otto Kade, eds. *Neue Beiträge zu Grundfragen der Übersetzungswissenschaft.* Beiheft 3 of *Fremdsprachen.* Leipzig: Enzyklopädie, 1973.

Newmark, Peter. *Approaches to Translation.* Oxford: Pergamon, 1981.

———. "Communicative and Semantic Translation." *Babel* 23 (1977): 163–77.

———. *A Textbook of Translation.* London: Prentice, 1988.

———. "Thought, Speech, and Translation." *Babel* 24 (1978): 127–29.

———. "Twenty-Three Restricted Rules of Translation." *Incorporated Linguist* 12 (1973): 9–15.

Nida, Eugene A. "A Framework for the Analysis and Evaluation of Theories of Translation." Brislin 46–79.

———. *Language Structure and Translation: Essays.* Stanford: Stanford UP, 1975.

———. "Linguistics and Ethnology in Translation Problems." *Word* 1-2 (1945): 194–208.

———. "Science of Translation." *Language* 45 (1969): 483–98.

———. "The Setting of Communication: A Largely Overlooked Factor in Translation." *Babel* 24 (1978): 114–17.

———. *Toward a Science of Translating.* Leiden: Brill, 1964.

Nida, Eugene A., and William D. Reyburn. *Meaning across Cultures.* New York: Amer. Missionary Soc., 1981.

Nida, Eugene A., and Charles R. Taber. *The Theory and Practice of Translation.* Leiden: Brill, 1974.

Nida, Eugene A., and Jan de Waard. *From One Language to Another.* Camden: Nelson, 1986.

Niedzielski, H. "Metalinguistics, Semantics and Idiomatic Expressions." Wilss and Thomé 154–64.

Nord, Christiane. *Textanalyse und Übersetzen.* Heidelberg: Groos, 1988.

Norton, Glyn P. *The Ideology and Language of Translation in Renaissance France.* Geneva: Droz, 1984.

Olmsted, Hugh M. *Translation and Translating: A Selective Bibliography of Bibliographies, Indexes, and Guides.* Binghamton: Center for Translation and Intercultural Communication, State U of New York, 1975.

Ortega y Gasset, José. "Miseria y esplendor de la traducción." *Obras completas.* Vol. 5. Madrid: Revista del Occidente, 1966. 431–52.

Otal Campo, José Luis. "Tendencias actuales en la teoría de la traducción." *Actas del Primer Congreso Nacional de Linguistica Aplicada.* Madrid: SGEL, 1983. 267–76.

Paepcke, Fritz. *Im Übersetzen leben.* Ed. Klaus Berger and Hans M. Speier. Tübingen: Narr, 1986.

Paker, Saliha. "Translated European Literature in the Late Ottoman Literary Polysystem." Hermans, *Literary* 67–82.

Paz, Octavio. "Lectura y contemplación." *Tradução e Communicação* 5 (1984): 7–38.

———. *Traducción: Literatura y literalidad.* Barcelona: Tusquets, 1971.

Poisson, Jacques. "La traduction, facteur d'acculturation." Horguelin 281–91.

Poltermann, Andreas. "Die Erfindung des Originals: Zur Geschichte der Übersetzungskonzeptionen in Deutschland im achtzehnten Jahrhundert." Schulze, *Literarische* 15–42.

Popovic, Anton. "Aspects of Metatext." *Canadian Review of Comparative Literature* 3 (1976): 225–35.

———. *Dictionary for the Analysis of Literary Translation.* Edmonton, AB: Dept. of Compar. Lit., U of Alberta, 1976.

———. "Die Stellung der Übersetzungstheorie im System der Literaturwissenschaft." *Slavica Slovaca* 7 (1972): 378–95.

———. "Translation Analysis and Literary History: A Slovak Approach to the Problem." *Babel* 14 (1968): 68–76.

———. "Übersetzung als Kommunikation." Popovic and Denes 5–24.

Popovic, Anton, and Imrich Denes. *Translation as Comparison.* Nitra, Czech.: Dept. of Compar. Lit., Pedagogical Fac., 1977.

Poulson, Sven-Olaf, and Wolfram Wilss, eds. *Angewandte Übersetzungswissenschaft.* Arhus: Wirtschaftsuniversität, 1980.

Pramod Talgeri, and S. B. Verma, eds. *Literature in Translation.* London: Sangam, 1988.

Premio Città di Monselice per una traduzione letteraria 3. Padua: Antoniana, 1974.

Primer Simposio Internacional sobre el Traductor y la Traducción. Madrid: APETI, 1982.

Problèmes littéraires de la traduction. Leiden: Brill, 1975.

Prochazka, Vladimir. "Notes on Translating Technique." *A Prague School Reader in Esthetics, Literary Structure, and Style.* Ed. Paul Garvin. Washington: Georgetown UP, 1955. 93–112.

Pucciarelli, Elsa T. de. *¿Que es la traducción?* Buenos Aires: Columba, 1970.

Rado, György. "Outline of a Systematic Translatology." *Babel* 25 (1979): 186–96.

———. "Scholars Approach Translation." *Babel* 30 (1984): 174–80.

Raffel, Burton. *The Art of Translating Poetry.* University Park: Pennsylvania State UP, 1988.

———. *The Forked Tongue: A Study of the Translation Process.* The Hague: Mouton, 1971.

Ray, Lila. "Multi-dimension Translation: Poetry." Brislin 261–78.

Reck, Michael, Jorge Enjuto, and Jorge Delacre. *Tres conferencias sobre la traducción.* Río Piedras: U de Puerto Rico, 1971.

Reese, Walter. *Literarische Rezeption.* Stuttgart: Metzler, 1980.

Reiss, Katharina. "Elend und Glanz der Übersetzung." *Europäische Mehrsprachigkeit.* Ed. Wolfgang Pöckl. Tübingen: Niemeyer, 1981. 409–19.

———. "Die literarische Übersetzung als Kommunikationsleistung." *Imago linguae: Beiträge zu Sprache, Deutung, und Übersetzen.* Ed. Karl-Heinz Bender, Karl Berger, and Mario Wandruszka. Munich: Fink, 1977. 487–501.

———. *Möglichkeiten und Grenzen der Übersetzungskritik.* Munich: Hueber, 1971.

———. "Quality in Translation; oder, Wann ist eine Übersetzung gut?" *Babel* 13 (1967): 199–208.

———. *Texttyp und Übersetzungsmethode.* Kronberg: Scriptor, 1976.

———. "Type, Kind and Individuality of Text." Even-Zohar and Toury 121–31.

———. "Der Übersetzungsvergleich." *Kontrastive Linguistik und Übersetzungswissenschaft.* Ed. Wolfgang Kühlwein, Gisela Thomé, and Wolfram Wilss. Munich: Fink, 1981. 311–19.

Reiss, Katharina, and Hans J. Vermeer. *Grundlegung einer allgemeinen Translationstheorie.* Tübingen: Niemeyer, 1984.

Rener, Frederick M. *Interpretation.* Amsterdam: Rodopi, 1989.

Reyburn, William D. "Cultural Equivalences and Non-equivalences in Translation." *Bible Translator* 20 (1969): 158–67.

Richards, Ivor A. "Toward a Theory of Translation." *Studies in Chinese Thought.* Ed. Arthur F. Wright. Chicago: U of Chicago P, 1967. 247–62.

Roberts, Roda P. "Translation: An Act of Communication." *Bulletin d'ACLA* 3 (1981): 151–63.

Rose, Marilyn Gaddis. "Time and Space in the Translation Process." Rose, *Translation Spectrum* 1–7.

———, ed. *Translation Excellence: Assessment, Achievement, Maintenance.* American Translators Association Scholarly Monograph Series 1. Binghamton: Center for Translation and Intercultural Communication, State U of New York P, 1987. 11–77.

———, ed. *Translation in the Humanities.* Binghamton: State U of New York P, 1977.

———, ed. *Translation Perspectives.* Binghamton: State U of New York P, 1984.

———, ed. *Translation Spectrum.* Albany: State U of New York P, 1981.

———. "Translation Types and Conventions." Rose, *Translation Spectrum* 31–40.

Ross, Richard B., ed. *Ten Papers on Translation.* Singapore: Occasional Papers of the Seameo Regional Language Center, 1982.

Saez Hermosilla, Teodoro. "Discurso y texto en el proceso de traducción." *Tradução e Communicação* 6 (1985): 113–30.

Sanchez de Zavalo, Victor. "Sobre la teoría de la traducción." *Márgenes* 1-2 (1980): 27–44.

Santoyo, Julio César. *La cultura traducida.* León, Sp.: U de León, 1983.

———— . *El delito de traducir.* León, Sp.: U de León, 1985.

———— . *Traducción, traducciones, traductores: Ensayo de bibliografía española.* León, Sp.: U de León, 1987.

Sanz Franco, Francisco. "La traducción antropólogico-cultural de los textos antiguos." *Emérita* 36 (1968): 57–76.

Schmidt, Denis J., ed. *Hermeneutics and the Poetic Motion.* Binghamton: Center for Translation and Intercultural Communication, State U of New York P, 1990.

Schogt, Henry G. *Linguistics, Literary Analysis and Literary Translation.* Toronto: U of Toronto P, 1988.

———— . "Semantic Theory and Translation Theory." *Texte* 4 (1986): 151–59.

Schulze, Brigitte, ed. *Die literarische Übersetzung: Fallstudien zu ihrer Kulturgeschichte.* Berlin: Schmidt, 1987.

———— . "Theorie der Dramenübersetzung—1960 bis heute." *Forum modernes Theater* 2 (1987): 1–17.

Sdun, Winfried. *Probleme und Theorien des Übersetzens.* Munich: Hueber, 1967.

Seleskovitch, Danica. "Pour une théorie de la traduction inspirée de sa pratique." *Meta* 25 (1980): 401–08.

———— . "Recherche universitaire et théorie interprétive de la traduction." *Meta* 26 (1981): 304–08.

———— . "Traduire: De l'expérience aux concepts." *Etudes de linguistique appliquée* 24 (1976): 64–91.

———— . "Vision du monde et traduction." *Etudes de linguistique appliquée* 12 (1973): 105–09.

Seleskovitch, Danica, and Marianne Lederer. *Interpréter pour traduire.* Paris: Didier, 1984.

Senger, Anneliese. *Deutsche Übersetzungstheorie im achtzehnten Jahrhundert.* Bonn: Bouvier, 1971.

Shaffer, Elinor, ed. *Translation.* Spec. issue of *Comparative Criticism* 6 (1984): ix–xxvii, 3–375.

Shavit, Zohar. "Translation of Children's Literature as a Function of Its Position in the Literary Polysystem." Even-Zohar and Toury 171–79.

Simon, Sherry, ed. "Conflits de jurisdiction: La double signature du texte traduit." *Meta* 34 (1989): 195–204.

Simpson, Ekundayo. "Methodology in Translation Criticism." *Meta* 20 (1975): 251–62.

———— . "Translating for National Integration." *Babel* 30 (1984): 26–33.

———— . "Translation and the Socio-cultural Problems of Developing Countries." *Babel* 26 (1980): 14–18.

———— . "Translation and Value Judgment." *Meta* 23 (1978): 211–19.

Snell-Hornby, Mary. "Dimension and Perspective in Literary Translation." Wilss and Thomé 105–13.

———— . *Translation Studies: An Integrated Approach.* Amsterdam: Benjamins, 1988.

———— . "Übersetzen, Sprache, Kultur." Snell-Hornby, *Übersetzungswissenschaft* 9–29.

————, ed. *Übersetzungswissenschaft—Eine Neuorientierung.* Tübingen: Francke, 1986.

Söll, Ludwig. "Sprachstruktur und Übersetzbarkeit." *Neusprachliche Mitteilungen* 31 (1968): 161–67.

———— . "Traduisibilité et intraduisibilité." *Meta* 16 (1971): 25–31.

Stackelberg, Jürgen von. *Literarische Rezeptionsformen: Übersetzung, Supplement, Parodie.* Frankfurt: Athenäum, 1972.

———— . *Übersetzungen aus zweiter Hand: Rezeptionsvorgänge in der europäischen Literatur vom vierzehnten bis zum achtzehnten Jahrhundert.* Berlin: De Gruyter, 1984.

Stein, Dieter. *Theoretische Grundlagen der Übersetzungswissenschaft.* Tübingen: Narr, 1980.

Steiner, George. *After Babel: Aspects of Language and Translation.* Oxford: Oxford UP, 1975.

Sternberg, Meir. "Polylingualism as Reality and Translation as Mimesis." Even-Zohar and Toury 221–39.

Stolze, Radegundis. *Grundlagen der Textübersetzung.* Heidelberg: Groos, 1982.

Störig, Hans Joachim, ed. *Das Problem des Übersetzens.* Darmstadt: Wissenschaftliche, 1963.

Studien zur Übersetzungswissenschaft. Beiheft 2 of *Fremdsprachen.* Leipzig: Enzyklopädie, 1971.

Svejcer, Aleksandr. *Übersetzung und Linguistik.* Berlin: Akademie, 1987.

Taber, Charles R. "Sociolinguistic Obstacles to Communication through Translation." *Meta* 25 (1980): 421–29.

Tatilon, Claude. "Le traducteur face au problème de la quadrature du style." *Cahiers de linguistique, d'orientalisme et de slavistique* 5-6 (1975): 405–14.

Terracini, Benvenuto. *Il problema della traduzione.* Ed. Bice Mortara Garaveli. Milan: Serra, 1983.

Thiel, Gisela. "Überlegungen zur übersetzungsrelevanten Textanalyse." Wilss, *Übersetzungswissenschaft* 367–84.

Tomlinson, Charles. "The Presence of Translation: A View of English Poetry." Warren 258–76.

Tosh, Wayne. *Syntactic Translation.* The Hague: Mouton, 1965.

Toury, Gideon. "Communication in Translated Texts: A Semiotic Approach." Wilss, *Semiotik* 99–109.

———— . *In Search of a Theory of Translation.* Tel Aviv: Porter Inst. for Poetics and Semiotics, 1980.

———— . "The Notion of 'Native Translator' and Translation Teaching." Wilss and Thomé 105–13.

———— . "A Rationale for Descriptive Translation Studies." *Dispositio* 7 (1982): 23–49.

———— . "Translated Literature: System, Norm, Performance. Toward a TT-Oriented Approach to Literary Translation." Even-Zohar and Toury 9–27.

————. "Translation, Literary Translation and Pseudotranslation." Shaffer 73–85.

————. "Translation: Theory and Practice." *Modern Poetry in Translation* 41-42 (1981): 3–12.

————. "The Translator as a Nonconformist-to-be; or, How to Train Translators So As to Violate Translational Norms." Poulson 180–94.

La traduction en jeu. Paris: Seghers-Laffont, 1974.

La traduzione, saggi e studi. Trieste: Centro per lo studio dell'insegnamento all'estro dell'italiano, 1973.

Transformer/traduire. Paris: Seghers-Laffont, 1973.

Tur, Jaume. "Sobre la teoría de la traducción." *Thesaurus* 29 (1974): 1–19.

Tymoczko, Thomas. "Translation and Meaning." Guenthner and Guenthner-Reutter 29–44.

Ure, Jean. "Types of Translation and Translationability." *Babel* 10 (1964): 5–11.

Vanderauwera, Ria. *Fiction in Translation: Policies and Options.* Amsterdam: Rodopi, 1985.

Vazquez-Ayora, Gerardo. *Introducción a la traductología.* Washington: Georgetown UP, 1977.

————. "On the Notion of an Analytical Unit of Translation." *Babel* 28 (1982): 70–81.

Venuti, Lawrence. "The Translator's Invisibility." *Criticism* 28 (1986): 179–211.

Vermeer, Hans J. *Aufsätze zur Translationstheorie.* Heidelberg: Inst. für Übersetzen und Dolmetschen, U of Heidelberg, 1983.

————. *Skopos und Translationsauftrag.* Ed. Margret Amman. Heidelberg: Inst. für Übersetzen und Dolmetschen, U of Heidelberg, 1989.

————. "Sprache und Kulturanthropologie." *Jahrbuch Deutsch als Fremdsprache* 4 (1978): 1–21.

————. "Übersetzen als kultureller Transfer." Snell-Hornby, *Übersetzungswissenschaft* 30–53.

Vernay, Henri. "Elemente einer Übersetzungswissenschaft." Kapp, *Übersetzer* 26–37.

Vinay, Jean-Paul. "Regards sur l'évolution des théories de la traduction depuis vingt ans." *Meta* 20 (1975): 7–27.

————. "La traduction humaine." *Le langage.* Ed. André Martinet. Paris: Gallimard, 1968. 729–57.

————. "La traduction littéraire est-elle un genre à part?" *Meta* 14 (1969): 5–21.

Vinay, Jean-Paul, and Jean Darbelnet. *Stylistique comparée du français et de l'anglais: Méthode de traduction.* Paris: Didier; Montreal: Beauchemin, 1971.

Warren, Rosanna, ed. *The Art of Translation.* Boston: Northeastern UP, 1989.

Weissman, Stanley Norman. *Foundations of a Theory of Translation for Natural Languages.* New York: Columbia UP, 1965.

Westerweel, Bart, and Theo D'haen, eds. *Something Understood: Studies in Anglo-Dutch Literary Translation.* Amsterdam: Rodopi, 1990.

Wilss, Wolfram. *Kognition und Übersetzen.* Tübingen: Niemeyer, 1988.

──── . *The Science of Translation.* Tübingen: Narr, 1982.

──── , ed. *Semiotik und Übersetzen.* Tübingen: Narr, 1980.

──── . "Topical Issues in Translator Training at Universities." *Translator and Interpreter Training and Foreign Language Pedagogy Strategy.* Ed. Peter W. Krawutschke. American Translators Association Scholarly Monograph Series 3. Binghamton: Center for Translation and Intercultural Communication, State U of New York P, 1989. 89–99.

──── , ed. *Übersetzungswissenschaft.* Darmstadt: Wissenschaftliche, 1981.

Wilss, Wolfram, and Gisela Thomé, eds. *Die Theorie des Übersetzens und ihr Aufschlusswert für die Übersetzungs- und Dolmetschdidaktik/Translation Theory and Its Implementation in the Teaching of Translating and Interpreting.* Tübingen: Narr, 1984.

Woodsworth, Judith, and Sherry Simon, eds. *La traduction et son public.* Spec. issue of *TTR* 1.2 (1988): 7–196.

Wuthenow, Ralph Rainer. *Das fremde Kunstwerk: Aspekte der literarischen Übersetzung.* Göttingen: Vandenhoeck, 1969.

Zapulla, Giuseppe. "Problemi e metodi di traduzione di poesia." *Idea* 20 (1964): 84–90.

Zierer, Ernesto. *Algunos conceptos básicos de la ciencia de la traducción.* Trujillo, Dom. Rep.: U Nacional de Trujillo, 1979.

Zlateva, Palma. "Translation: Text and Pre-Text. 'Adequacy' and 'Acceptability' in Crosscultural Communication." Bassnett and Lefevere 29–37.

Zuber, Roger. *Les "Belles infidèles" et la formation du goût classique.* Paris: Colin, 1968.

Zuber-Skerritt, Ortrun, ed. *The Languages of Theatre: Problems in the Translation and Transposition of Drama.* Oxford: Pergamon, 1980.

──── . *Page to Stage: Theatre as Translation.* Amsterdam: Rodopi, 1984.

Index

Addison, Joseph, 40
Aiken W. A., 99–100, 101, 102, 103, 104–05, 106
Amyot, Jacques, 121
Anderson, Sherwood, 82
Ariosto, Ludovico, 121
Aristophanes, 16, 21, 25, 27, 28–29, 37, 38, 40–41, 44, 47–48, 54–55, 65–66, 83
Auden, W. H., 67–68, 121–22
Augustine, Saint, 131

Baudissin, Count Wolf, 121
Beckett, Samuel, 52, 57, 80
Benson, Stella, 20
Betjeman, John, 60
Bible, 6, 8, 22–23, 59, 89, 114, 118, 120, 121, 126, 131, 135, 143, 144. *See also* Septuagint; Vulgate
Blake, William, 137, 138
Brode, Anthony, 47, 80–81
Browning, Robert, 26, 43, 102
Bühler, Karl, 9
Burns, Robert, 57, 69–70, 76–77
Burton, Sir Richard, 98–99, 105
Butler, Samuel, 16, 24–25
Byron, George Gordon, Lord, 24, 27, 45–46, 58–59, 72–73, 82, 124, 125

Calverly, C. S., 59
Carlyle, Joseph D., 127
Carroll, Lewis, 56, 71, 73–74
Catford, John C., 8
Catullus, 16, 33–34, 42, 74–75, 77, 79–80, 89–108, 129
Chatterton, Thomas, 122
Chesterton, G. K., 46, 69
Chikamatsu, Monzaemon, 13, 31
Cicero, 123
Clough, Arthur Hugh, 29–30
Coleridge, Hartley, 46
Conrad, Joseph, 21, 62, 63, 64

Cooke, Rose Terry, 22–23, 68–69, 82–83
Copley, F. O., 98, 100, 102
Cowell, E. B., 119
Crane, Stephen, 66–67

Dante, Alighieri, 70
d'Alembert, Jean le Rond, 130
De la Mare, Walter, 56
Delille, Abbé, 130
Dickens, Charles, 61
Dickinson, Patrick, 48, 66, 83
Dobson, Austin, 25–26
Dos Passos, John, 38, 40, 41, 72
Dryden, John, 26, 62
Du Bellay, Joachim, 117

Eliot, T. S., 48
Ellis, Collin, 53–54
Ellis, E. J., 137–38
Euripides, 29, 47–48
Even-Zohar, Itamar, 11

Faulkner, William, 69
Fedorov, Andrei V., 7
Feng Chi, 72, 124
Ferguson, Sir Samuel, 124
Fitts, Dudley, 38–39
FitzGerald, Edward, 119–20, 128, 145
Forster, E. M., 65
Freeman, Mary E. Wilkins, 50
Frere, John Hookhan, 124

Gardner, Earle Stanley, 43–44
Garland, Hamlin, 39, 50
Gay, John, 36
Gilchrist, Alexander, 137, 138
Goethe, Johann Wolfgang von, 19, 116, 124, 125, 144
Goold, George P., 105
Gottsched, Johann Christoph, 130
Grainger, James, 101, 102, 104, 106
Graves, Robert, 41, 78

Gregory, Horace, 78, 98, 102–03, 105, 108

Hardy, Thomas, 28, 57, 64
Harington, John, 121
Harrison, T. W., 37
Hawthorne, Nathaniel, 32, 39, 61–62
Henry, O., 35
Herder, Johann Gottfried, 119
Hickie, W. J., 25
Homer, 95, 119, 124, 128.
Hood, Thomas, 53, 60
Hopkins, Gerard Manley, 47, 50
Horace, 131
House, Juliane, 9–10
Houseman, Lawrence, 51, 55
Housman, A. E., 32–33, 48–49
Huetius, Petrus Danielus, 121
Hugo, Victor, 125
Hull, William, 42

Ibsen, Henrik, 123

James, Henry, 39, 79
Jerome, 126, 131
John of Trevisa, 116

Keats, John, 35–36, 43–44
Kelly, W. K., 75, 80, 101, 102
Khayyám, Omar, 138. *See also* FitzGerald, Edward

Labid, 127
Lamb, George, 101, 102, 104, 106
Larkin, Philip, 26
Lawrence, D. H., 26, 36
Lear, Edward, 33, 34–35
Leigh, Henry S., 28
Leland, C. G., 68
Le Tourneur, Pierre, 144
Levy, Jiri, 11
Lindsay, Jack, 39, 40, 44, 83, 98, 103
London, Jack, 51, 63
Luther, Martin, 8, 126, 144.

Manyoshu, 22
Martin, Theodore, 42, 74–75
McLeish, K., 80, 93, 94, 99, 104
McPherson, James, 122, 144

Melville, Herman, 9, 23–24
Meredith, George, 21, 25, 42, 57, 59–60
Michie, James, 42, 77–78, 103, 107
Mills, Barriss, 42, 103, 106
Milton, John, 145–46
Moss, Howard, 42
Meyers, R., 98, 107–08

Nash, Ogden, 43–44, 80
Newmark, Peter, 10, 11
Nida, Eugene A., 7, 8
Nyerere, Julius, 124

O'Flaherty, Liam, 64
Ormsby, R. J., 98, 107–08
Ovid, 124

Parker, Douglass, 27, 39, 55, 83
Pauker, Ted, 32, 41
Peacock, Thomas Love, 23
Percy, Thomas, 122
Perkins, David, 124
Plutarch, 121
Poe, Edgar Allan, 64, 65
Pope, Alexander, 23
Popovic, Anton, 11, 13
Pound, Ezra, 129
Praed, W. M., 82
Prévost, Abbé, 118, 119
Pulci, Luigi, 124

Qur'an, 120

Raphael, Frederick, 80, 93, 94, 99, 104
Reiss, Katharina, 9
Retzsch, Maurice, 125
Rhys, Jean, 31
Richardson, Samuel, 118, 119
Rogers, Benjamin, 22, 27, 48
Roscommon, William, earl of, 117

St. Gelais, Octavien de, 124
Sappho, 110, 129
Schlegel, Dorothea, 121
Septuagint, 114, 115, 121
Sesar, Carl, 42, 99, 103
Shakespeare, William, 27–28, 30, 70, 121, 124, 143

Shih ching, 22
Simmons, J., 37
Sisson, C. H., 98, 105, 107
Smith, Stevie, 77
Smith, W. H., 25
Smithers, L. C., 105, 107
Snell-Hornby, Mary, 10
Sommerstein, Alan, 40, 48, 51, 66, 83
Sophocles, 13, 28, 49
Staël, Mme de, 125
Steele, Richard, 40
Steiner, George, 11
Stevenson, Robert Louis, 23, 37, 54, 63, 79
Stowe, Harriet Beecher, 39
Strindberg, August, 123
Sutherland, Donald, 29, 41, 66, 83
Swanson, R. A., 98, 103
Swift, Jonathan, 20, 73
Swinburne, Algernon Charles, 21, 137, 138
Symons, Arthur, 78

Taylor, Bayard, 38
Tende, Gaspard de, 130
Thackeray, William Makepeace, 35, 61
Thomas, Dylan, 38
Thwaite, Anthony, 30

Tieck, Ludwig, 121
Toury, Gideon, 10
Tremenheere, J. H. A., 42, 77–78
Turner, Godfrey, 40

Vergil, 116–17
Villon, François, 70, 129
Voss, Johann Heinrich, 124

Walpole, Horace, 122–23
Way, Arthur S., 25, 40, 83
Wender, Dorothea, 99, 103
Wesley, Samuel, 28
Wharton, Edith, 50
Wheelwright, Arthur, 40–41
Whigham, Peter, 42, 98, 99, 103, 106, 108
Whitman, Walt, 46
Wodehouse, P. G., 43
Woolf, Virginia, 27
Wordsworth, William, 46
Wright, F. A., 100, 104

Yeats, William Butler, 124, 138
Young, Edward, 144

Zukofsky, Celia, 77, 96–97, 99
Zukofsky, Louis, 77, 96–97, 99